Steffen Heinzl

Policies for Web Services

Steffen Heinzl

Policies for Web Services

Improving the Description of Services

Südwestdeutscher Verlag für Hochschulschriften

Impressum/Imprint (nur für Deutschland/ only for Germany)
Bibliografische Information der Deutschen Nationalbibliothek: Die Deutsche Nationalbibliothek verzeichnet diese Publikation in der Deutschen Nationalbibliografie; detaillierte bibliografische Daten sind im Internet über http://dnb.d-nb.de abrufbar.
Alle in diesem Buch genannten Marken und Produktnamen unterliegen warenzeichen-, marken- oder patentrechtlichem Schutz bzw. sind Warenzeichen oder eingetragene Warenzeichen der jeweiligen Inhaber. Die Wiedergabe von Marken, Produktnamen, Gebrauchsnamen, Handelsnamen, Warenbezeichnungen u.s.w. in diesem Werk berechtigt auch ohne besondere Kennzeichnung nicht zu der Annahme, dass solche Namen im Sinne der Warenzeichen- und Markenschutzgesetzgebung als frei zu betrachten wären und daher von jedermann benutzt werden dürften.

Verlag: Südwestdeutscher Verlag für Hochschulschriften Aktiengesellschaft & Co. KG
Dudweiler Landstr. 99, 66123 Saarbrücken, Deutschland
Telefon +49 681 37 20 271-1, Telefax +49 681 37 20 271-0
Email: info@svh-verlag.de
Zugl.: Marburg, Philipps-Universität, Diss., 2009

Herstellung in Deutschland:
Schaltungsdienst Lange o.H.G., Berlin
Books on Demand GmbH, Norderstedt
Reha GmbH, Saarbrücken
Amazon Distribution GmbH, Leipzig
ISBN: 978-3-8381-1446-0

Imprint (only for USA, GB)
Bibliographic information published by the Deutsche Nationalbibliothek: The Deutsche Nationalbibliothek lists this publication in the Deutsche Nationalbibliografie; detailed bibliographic data are available in the Internet at http://dnb.d-nb.de.
Any brand names and product names mentioned in this book are subject to trademark, brand or patent protection and are trademarks or registered trademarks of their respective holders. The use of brand names, product names, common names, trade names, product descriptions etc. even without a particular marking in this works is in no way to be construed to mean that such names may be regarded as unrestricted in respect of trademark and brand protection legislation and could thus be used by anyone.

Publisher: Südwestdeutscher Verlag für Hochschulschriften Aktiengesellschaft & Co. KG
Dudweiler Landstr. 99, 66123 Saarbrücken, Germany
Phone +49 681 37 20 271-1, Fax +49 681 37 20 271-0
Email: info@svh-verlag.de

Printed in the U.S.A.
Printed in the U.K. by (see last page)
ISBN: 978-3-8381-1446-0

Copyright © 2010 by the author and Südwestdeutscher Verlag für Hochschulschriften Aktiengesellschaft & Co. KG and licensors
All rights reserved. Saarbrücken 2010

Abstract

Web services are predominantly used to implement service-oriented architectures (SOA). However, there are several areas such as temporal dimensions, real-time, streaming, or efficient and flexible file transfers where web service functionality should be extended. These extensions can, for example, be achieved by using policies. Since there are often alternative solutions to provide functionality (e.g., different protocols can be used to achieve the transfer of data), the WS-Policy standard is especially useful to extend web services with policies. It allows to create policies to generally state the properties under which a service is provided and to explicitly express alternative properties. To extend the functionality of web services, two policies are introduced in this thesis: the Temporal Policy and the Communication Policy.

The temporal policy is the foundation for adding temporal dimensions to a WS-Policy. The temporal policy itself is not a WS-Policy but an independent policy language that describes temporal dimensions of and dependencies between temporal policies and WS-Policies. Switching of protocol dependencies, pricing of services, quality of service, and security are example areas for using a temporal policy. To describe protocol dependencies of a service for streaming, real-time and file transfers, a communication policy can be utilized. The communication policy is a concrete WS-Policy. With the communication policy, a service can expose the protocols it depends on for a communication *after* its invocation. Thus, a web service client knows the protocols required to support a communication with the service. Therefore, it is possible to evaluate beforehand whether an invocation of a service is reasonable. On top of the newly introduced policies, novel mechanisms and tools are provided to alleviate service use and enable flexible and efficient data handling. Furthermore, the involvement of the end user in the development process can be achieved more easily.

The Flex-SwA architecture, the first component in this thesis based on the newly introduced policies, implements the actual file transfers and streaming protocols that are described as dependencies in a communication policy. Several communication patterns support the flexible handling of the communication. A reference concept enables seamless message forwarding with reduced data movement.

Based on the Flex-SwA implementation and the communication policy, it is possible to improve usability—especially in the area of service-oriented Grids—by integrating data transfers into an automatically generated web and Grid service client. The Web and Grid Service Browser is introduced in this thesis as such a generic client. It provides a familiar environment for using services by offering the client generation as part of the browser. Data transfers are directly integrated into service invocation without having to perform data transmissions explicitly. For multimedia MIME types, special plugins allow the consumption of multimedia data.

To enable an end user to build applications that also leverage high performance computing resources, the Service-enabled Mashup Editor is presented that lets the user combine popular web applications with web and Grid services. Again, the communication policy provides descriptive means for file transfers and Flex-SwA's reference concept is used for data exchange.

To show the applicability of these novel concepts, several use cases from the area of multimedia processing have been selected. Based on the temporal policy, the communication policy, Flex-SwA, the Web and Grid Service Browser, and the Service-enabled Mashup Editor, the development of a scalable service-oriented multimedia architecture is presented. The multimedia SOA offers, among others, a face detection workflow, a video-on-demand service, and an audio resynthesis service. More precisely, a video-on-demand service describes its dependency on a multicast protocol by using a communication policy. A temporal policy is then used to perform the description of a protocol switch from one multicast protocol to another one by changing the communication policy at the end of its validity period. The Service-enabled Mashup Editor is used as a client for the new multicast protocol after the multicast protocol has been switched. To stream single frames from a frame decoder service to a face detection service (which are both part of the face detection workflow) and to transfer audio files with the different Flex-SwA communication patterns to an audio resynthesis service, Flex-SwA is used. The invocation of the face detection workflow and the audio resynthesis service is realized with the Web and Grid Service Browser.

Zusammenfassung

Web Services sind die vorherrschende Technologie zur Entwicklung service-orientierter Architekturen (SOA). Jedoch sollte die Funktionalität in einigen Gebieten (zeitliche Dimensionen, Echtzeit, Streaming oder bei effizienten und flexiblen Datenübertragungen) erweitert werden. Die Erweiterungen können beispielsweise durch Policies realisiert werden. Da es oft verschiedene Möglichkeiten gibt, eine Funktionalität zu erweitern (z.B. mehrere Protokolle zur Übertragung von Daten), bietet sich zur Beschreibung WS-Policy an. WS-Policy erlaubt die Umsetzung konkreter Policies, die allgemein die Eigenschaften beschreiben, unter denen ein Service angeboten wird. Dabei ermöglicht eine Policy explizit die Auswahl zwischen alternativen Eigenschaften. Um die genannten Probleme zu behandeln, werden in dieser Arbeit zwei neue Policies eingeführt: Temporal Policy und Communication Policy.

Eine Temporal Policy ist die Grundlage, um WS-Policies eine zeitliche Dimension hinzuzufügen. Bei einer Temporal Policy handelt es sich nicht um eine WS-Policy, sondern um eine Policy Sprache, die zeitliche Dimensionen und Abhängigkeiten zwischen Temporal Policies und WS-Policies ausdrückt. Das Umschalten von Protokollabhängigkeiten, die Bepreisung von Services, Dienstgüte und Sicherheit sind einige Gebiete für den Einsatz von Temporal Policies. Um hingegen Protokollabhängigkeiten eines Services im Hinblick auf Echtzeit, Streaming und Datenübertragung zu beschreiben, wird die Communication Policy verwendet. Ein Service kann seine Protokollabhängigkeiten veröffentlichen, um einem Client mitzuteilen, wie er mit dem Service *nach* dessen Aufruf kommunizieren kann. Dadurch ist es für den Client möglich, im Vorfeld zu überprüfen, ob der Aufruf des Services sinnvoll ist. Aufbauend auf den Policies werden neue Mechanismen und Werkzeuge präsentiert, die die Verwendung von Services sowie die Durchführung von Datenübertragungen vereinfachen. Ferner kann der Servicebenutzer einfacher in den Entwicklungsprozess involviert werden.

Die Flex-SwA Architektur ist die erste Komponente dieser Arbeit, die auf den neu vorgestellten Policies aufbaut. Sie dient der Implementierung von Datenübertragungen und Streaming-Protokollen, die als Protokollabhängigkeiten durch eine Communication Policy beschrieben werden. Flex-SwA bietet mehrere Kommunikationsmuster an, die eine flexible Handhabung der Kommunikation ermöglichen. Ferner erlaubt die Verwendung eines Referenzkonzepts die einfache Weiterleitung von Daten mit reduziertem Datenumfang.

Mit Hilfe von Flex-SwA und der Communication Policy ist es möglich, die Benutzbarkeit – vor allem im Bereich service-orientierter Grids – zu verbessern, indem die Datenübertragung in einen automatisch generierten Web oder Grid Service Client integriert wird. Der Web und Grid Service Browser, der in dieser Arbeit vorgestellt wird, agiert als solch ein generischer Client. Durch den Web und Grid Service Browser wird dem Benutzer eine gewohnte Umgebung im Browser geboten. Die Datenübertragung wird direkt beim Service Aufruf gehandhabt, ohne den Transfer explizit veranlassen zu müssen. Durch spezielle Plugins können Multimediadaten veranschaulicht, angesehen oder angehört werden.

Um einem Benutzer die Erzeugung neuer Anwendungen, die auf Hochleistungsressourcen zurückgreifen, zu erlauben, wird ein Mashup Editor präsentiert, der den Anwender populäre Webanwendungen mit Web und Grid Services kombinieren lässt. Auch hier wird die Communication Policy zur Beschreibung von Datenübertragungen des Services benutzt. Flex-SwA setzt durch sein Referenzkonzept den Datenaustausch um.

Um die Anwendbarkeit, der in dieser Arbeit vorgestellten Konzepte zu zeigen, wurden einige Anwendungsfälle aus dem Multimediabereich ausgewählt. Basierend auf der Temporal Policy, der Communication Policy, Flex-SwA, dem Web und Grid Service Browser und dem Mashup Editor wird die Entwicklung einer Multimedia SOA präsentiert, die unter anderem einen Workflow für Gesichtserkennung, einen Video-on-demand Service und einen Audioresynthese-Service umfasst.

Konkret beschreibt der Video-on-demand Service seine Abhängigkeit zu einem Multicast-Protokoll durch eine Communication Policy. Anschließend wird eine Temporal Policy verwendet, um das Umschalten von einem Multicast-Protokoll zu einem anderen zu beschreiben, indem die Communication Policy am Ende ihres Gültigkeitszeitraumes ausgetauscht wird. Der Mashup Editor wird als Client für das neue Multicast-Protokoll nach der Umschaltung verwendet. Um Frames von einem Frame-Dekodierungsservices zu einem Service zur Gesichtserkennung zu senden und um Audiodateien mit den verschiedenen Flex-SwA Kommunikationsmustern zu einem Audioresynthese-Service zu übertragen, wird Flex-SwA verwendet. Der Aufruf des Workflows zur Gesichtserkennung und des Audioresynthese-Services wird mit Hilfe des Web und Grid Service Browsers umgesetzt.

Acknowledgements

I would like to thank Prof. Dr. Bernd Freisleben for his support and supervision during the time of this thesis, for sharing his vast knowledge, and for the discussions that always improved my work.

I would like to thank Prof. Dr. Thomas Barth from the University of Siegen for acting as a reviewer for my thesis.

Also, I would like to thank my past and present colleagues at the Distributed Systems Group, particularly Markus Mathes, Dr. Thomas Friese, Dominik Seiler, Ernst Juhnke, Thilo Stadelmann, Dr. Matthew Smith, Tim Dörnemann, Kay Dörnemann, Dr. Ralph Ewerth, Roland Schwarzkopf, and Christoph Stoidner.

Furthermore, I would like to thank Prof. Dr. Helmut Dohmann for his advice during my years of study and the support during the time of this thesis.

I would also like to thank my dear girlfriend Vanessa and my dear friends Christian Heil, Miriam Auth, Tanja Freitag, and Nancy Föllmer!

Last but not least, special thanks are dedicated to my family—especially my parents—for their support. You made all of this possible!

Danksagung

Ich möchte mich bei Herrn Prof. Dr. Bernd Freisleben für seine Unterstützung und die hevorragende Betreuung meiner Doktorarbeit bedanken wie auch für die zahlreichen Diskussionen, die meine Arbeiten noch weiter verbesserten.

Ich möchte mich bei Herrn Prof. Dr. Thomas Barth von der Universität Siegen bedanken, dass er als Zweitgutachter für meine Doktorarbeit zur Verfügung steht.

Weiterhin bedanke ich mich bei meinen Kollegen der AG Verteilte Systeme, insbesondere bei Markus Mathes, Dr. Thomas Friese, Dominik Seiler, Ernst Juhnke, Thilo Stadelmann, Dr. Matthew Smith, Tim Dörnemann, Kay Dörnemann, Dr. Ralph Ewerth, Roland Schwarzkopf und Christoph Stoidner.

Auch bei Herrn Prof. Dr. Helmut Dohmann möchte ich mich für seine Hilfe und Ratschläge während meines Studiums und für die Unterstützung während meines Promotionsstudiums bedanken.

Bei meiner Freundin Vanessa und bei meinen Freunden Christian Heil, Miriam Auth, Tanja Freitag und Nancy Föllmer möchte ich mich herzlich bedanken!

Abschließend möchte ich mich bei meiner Familie – vor allem – bei meinen Eltern für ihre Hilfe und Unterstützung bedanken. Ohne euch wäre das nicht möglich gewesen!

Contents

1 Introduction   **1**
    1.1   Research Contributions   9
    1.2   Organization of the Thesis   13

2 Policies for Web Services   **15**
    2.1   Introduction   15
    2.2   Temporal Policy: Description of Temporal Dimensions   17
    2.3   Communication Policy: Description of Communication Options .   17
    2.4   Flex-SwA: Architecture for Data Handling   18
    2.5   Web and Grid Service Browser: Familiar Environment for Service Use   18
    2.6   Web and Grid Service-enabled Mashup Editor   19
    2.7   Summary   19

3 Describing Temporal Dimensions of Policies   **21**
    3.1   Introduction   21
    3.2   The Need for Dynamic Properties   22
    3.3   Temporal Policies   22
        3.3.1   WS-Policy   23
        3.3.2   Temporal Policy Schema   23
        3.3.3   Temporal Policy Referencing WS-Policies   26
        3.3.4   Actions and Event Handlers   26
    3.4   The Temporal Policy Runtime Environment   29
    3.5   Exposing Validity Dates to the Service User   31
    3.6   Summary   32

4 Defining Communication Options for Web Services   **33**
    4.1   Introduction   33
    4.2   Defining a Communication Policy   38
        4.2.1   Real-time or Streaming Requirements   39
        4.2.2   Legacy Integration   40
        4.2.3   Leveraging File Transfers   42
    4.3   Summary   44

5	**Facilitating Flexible Data Transfers**	**47**
	5.1 Introduction	47
	5.2 Web Service Interaction Patterns	48
	5.3 Flex-SwA Architecture	51
	5.3.1 Flex-SwA Protocol Stack	52
	5.3.2 Reference Concept	55
	5.3.3 Communication Patterns	56
	5.3.4 Memory Patterns	59
	5.3.5 Compatibility	59
	5.3.6 Protocol Decision	60
	5.3.7 Reduced Data Movement	60
	5.3.8 Seamless Message Forwarding	60
	5.4 Summary	62
6	**Enabling Simple Service Use**	**63**
	6.1 Introduction	63
	6.2 Supported Web Service Styles	65
	6.3 The Web and Grid Service Browser	66
	6.3.1 Grid Services Search Engine	67
	6.3.2 User Interface Generator Service	69
	6.3.3 Execution Engine	70
	6.3.4 Result Presentation and Visualization	70
	6.3.5 Rating System	70
	6.4 Summary	70
7	**Leveraging Grid Resources for End User Development**	**73**
	7.1 Introduction	73
	7.2 Mashup Editor Classification	74
	7.2.1 Environment	74
	7.2.2 Component Model	74
	7.2.3 Composition Model	75
	7.3 Service-enabled Mashup Editor	75
	7.3.1 Scalability	77
	7.3.2 Views	77
	7.3.3 Export to BPEL	78
	7.4 Summary	78
8	**Implementation**	**81**
	8.1 Introduction	81
	8.2 Introduction to the Apache Axis Framework	81
	8.3 XML2Java Model Generator	83
	8.4 Temporal Policy	83
	8.4.1 Temporal Policy Runtime Environment	84

	8.4.2	Integration of Policy Weaving into the Axis Framework	85
	8.4.3	Integrating the Temporal Policy Manager into a Servlet Engine	85
	8.4.4	Integrating the Temporal Policy Manager into the Globus Toolkit	87
8.5	Communication Policy	87
	8.5.1	Communication Policy Model	88
	8.5.2	Standalone Communication Policy	88
8.6	Flex-SwA	90
	8.6.1	Middleware Components	90
	8.6.2	Protocol Capabilities	91
	8.6.3	Buffers	92
	8.6.4	Threads	92
	8.6.5	Interaction	94
	8.6.6	Configuration of the Web Service Container	97
	8.6.7	Deploying a Flex-SwA Service	97
	8.6.8	Communication Policy Support in Flex-SwA	97
8.7	Web and Grid Service Browser	100
	8.7.1	Firefox Add-on	101
	8.7.2	Java Bridge	104
	8.7.3	Browser Overlay	104
	8.7.4	User Interface Generation	104
	8.7.5	Search Engine	106
	8.7.6	WSDL and XML Schema Parser	110
	8.7.7	HTML Structure	110
	8.7.8	Proxy Certificate Generation and Execution Engine	112
	8.7.9	Result Presentation Engine	112
8.8	Service-enabled Mashup Editor	112
	8.8.1	Extensibility	113
	8.8.2	Developer and User View	113
	8.8.3	Proxy	117
8.9	Summary	117

9 Evaluation — 119

9.1	Introduction		119
9.2	A Service-Oriented Architecture for Multimedia Processing		120
	9.2.1	General Roles in a Multimedia SOA	120
	9.2.2	Structure of a Multimedia Workflow	122
	9.2.3	Modeling the Data Flow in BPEL4WS	123
	9.2.4	Scalability	124
	9.2.5	Ease of Use	125
	9.2.6	Multimedia SOA Layer Model	125
9.3	Services of the Multimedia SOA		126

	9.3.1 Use Cases 129
	9.3.2 Implementation Issues 132
9.4	Quantitative Evaluation of the Use Cases 133
	9.4.1 Audio Resynthesis (WebVoice) 133
	9.4.2 Face Detection in Videos 137
	9.4.3 Video-on-Demand 141
9.5	Qualitative Evaluation of the Use Cases 145
	9.5.1 Audio Resynthesis (WebVoice) 145
	9.5.2 Face Detection in Videos 147
	9.5.3 Video on Demand 151
9.6	Summary 151

10 Related Work 157
10.1 Description of Temporal Dimensions 157
10.2 Definition of Communication Options for Web Services 158
10.3 Facilitating Flexible and Efficient Data Handling 160
10.4 Enabling Simple Service Use 161
10.5 Leveraging Grid Resources for End User Development 165
10.6 Frameworks for Service-oriented Multimedia Analysis 166

11 Conclusions and Future Work 169
11.1 Summary 169
11.2 Future Work 170

1
Introduction

Over the last decades, software systems have become more and more complex. Modular concepts, like functions, classes and objects, and lately aspects, have been introduced into the programming languages to better reflect real objects and processes. These concepts help to modularize the code written by developers. Each newly introduced concept can be used to create higher abstraction levels and better deal with the complexity of real-world objects. The idea of developing a robust architecture to allow fast, simple, and secure integration of entire systems and applications on disparate heterogeneous platforms has become popular ever since the Common Object Request Broker Architecture (CORBA) was introduced. This idea takes the code modularization concept one step further. Functions/methods can be invoked over a network. The architecture is independent of platforms, protocols, programming languages, devices, etc. But CORBA was not broadly adopted by the industry due to many reasons: for example, the high development effort for software, usability, the lack of HTTP binding and firewall tunneling capabilities, and the lack of standardization of the binary protocols used by the Object Request Brokers (ORB). CORBA's object-oriented concept rather reflects a developer's view than a business view on business processes. Some of the disadvantages have been resolved over time, but meanwhile the idea of service-oriented architectures (SOA) was introduced.

Web services are the predominant technology to implement SOAs and provide a rich set of features to organize IT infrastructures of companies, interoperable Grids for academia and industry, event-driven architectures, architectures for multimedia analysis, etc. They pursue the same goals as CORBA, but additionally focus more on a business view by using services instead of objects to represent business processes and on reachability over the network—more specifically—the Internet. Therefore, services cannot only be used internally in an institution (companies, universities, research facilities, etc.), but also between institutions and even—targeting a much broader audience—by Internet users. Web services are defined by the three core specifications

- SOAP (formerly known as Simple Object Access Protocol) [47] for message exchange,
- WSDL (Web Services Description Language) [29] for service description, and
- UDDI (Universal Description, Discovery, and Integration) [30] for service discovery.

They can be extended by many web services specifications (so-called WS-*) adding transactional behavior, security, etc. to web services. Grid services additionally extend web services by implementing the Web Services Resource Framework (WSRF) [46] to provide a standardized way to manage state in services. WSRF includes the management of resources, particularly the life cycle. By using web service standards, it is possible to interconnect heterogeneous Grids. WSRF additionally allows to, for example, query the state of a job by saving the job's state to a resource. In addition to resource management, mechanisms to *address* the resources holding the state information and to send notifications for long running jobs or service invocations are useful. These mechanisms are described by two additional web service specifications: WS-Addressing [48] and WS-Notification [4].

Figure 1.1 gives a general overview of web service specifications [58].

These specifications extend web services in the following areas:

- Resources: State is introduced into web services. Normally, web services are stateless, i.e. between two invocations the web service has no knowledge of the client invoking the service.

- Business processes: Business processes are presented as workflows of services, for example, via the Business Process Execution Language for Web Services (BPEL4WS).

- Security: Security and trust mechanisms like encryption, signing of messages, etc. are added.

- Metadata: Metadata are added to web services. This can be metadata in general (e.g., WS-Policy), metadata for service discovery (e.g., UDDI), or metadata for negotiating service agreements (e.g., WS-Agreement [16]).

- Messaging: Messaging specifications comprise, among others, SOAP for message exchange, SOAP Messages with Attachments (SwA) [20] for the

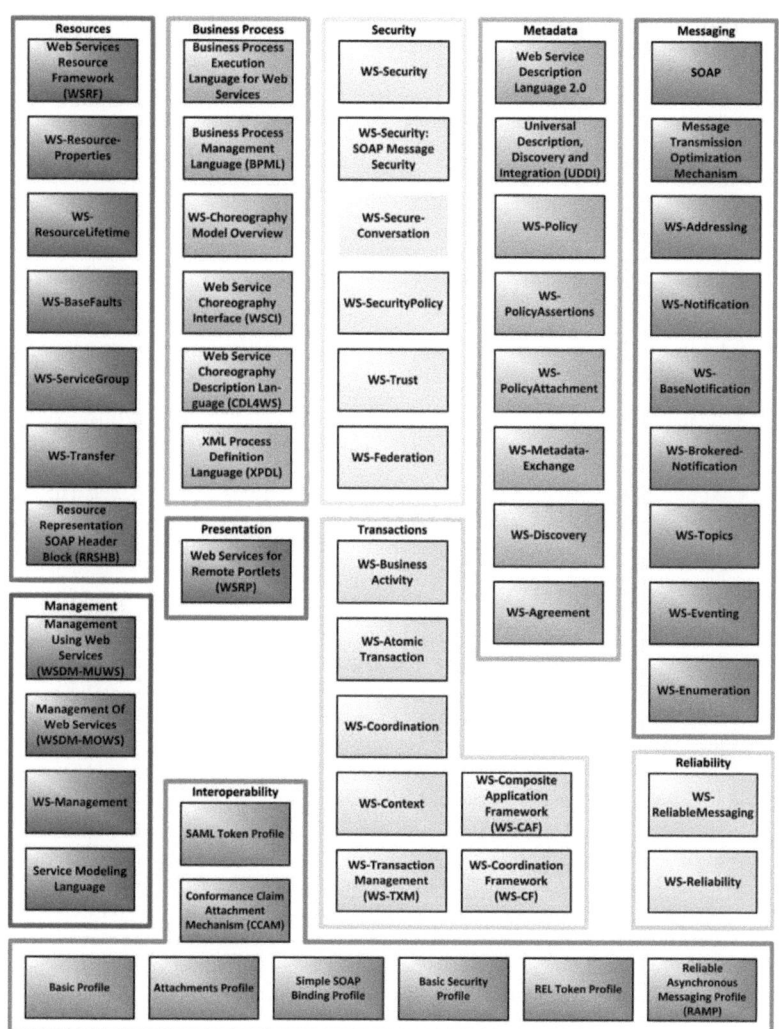

Figure 1.1: Overview of WS-Standards.

exchange of large amounts of data, and WS-Notification to allow web services clients to be notified when a web service has achieved a certain progress or finished execution.

- Management: Management specifications provide means to manage network resources locally or remotely via web services.

- Presentation: The Web Services Remote Portlet (WSRP) specification [64] defines how a user interface at a remote site can be included in a portal.

- Transactions: Transactional behaviour is added to web services.

- Reliability: The reliable transfer of messages is added to web services on the SOAP level.

- Interoperability: Interoperability specifications define which specifications interoperate with which versions.

Although there are many web service specifications, it is still hard to realize certain types of applications:

- Applications with high performance computing needs often encounter problems due to the time-consuming (and memory-consuming) SOAP encoding and due to the lengthy SOAP messages that result in longer data transfer times. These performance problems may either occur because large amounts of data have to be transferred or many messages have to be sent.

    For example, realizing a video-on-demand application with web services leads to performance problems due to the repetitive sending of SOAP messages. If the messages are delivered too slowly, a user might experience delays when watching the video. This can be partially resolved by buffering. But video multicasting, video conferences, or web conferences normally induce (soft) real-time constraints. To fulfill these constraints, it is reasonable to switch to protocols especially suited for such tasks.

    Different kind of applications often deal with large amounts of data and need much computational power, such that they leverage the computational power of the Grid. Examples are astrophysical applications (finding clusters, etc.), multimedia applications (face detection, etc.), and financial applications (Monte Carlo analysis to determine the price of options, etc.). Here, often large file transfers have to be handled in a user-friendly manner and efficient streaming of data has to be supported.

- Applications having dynamic properties that vary over time will result in an unstable service interface. A web service consists of functional and non-functional properties. The functional properties (like service name, port, operations, etc.) will not change over the time. If they change, a new service will be created. But non-functional properties like security configurations, price of a service, etc. might change more frequently. At the moment, changes in nonfunctional properties will leave the service uninvokable if service descriptions had been buffered.

If, for example, a company sets a price for the use of computational power of services, the pricing might change relatively often depending on usage, etc. The description of validity periods for the prices might be reasonable in this case. Urgent customer requests have to be handled directly whereas long running jobs might mainly be running during the night. Thus, pricing could occur according to day and night time, according to the current load on the compute nodes, etc. Swapping the service description every day would result in a highly unstable service.

Another example is today's manufacturing domain (e.g., vehicles, aircraft) where the software infrastructure is organized into three layers: business layer, intermediate layer, and manufacturing layer. The vertical adoption of service-orientation in the three layers is desirable, since it leads to a homogeneous communication infrastructure based on a single communication paradigm within the entire enterprise [60]. Using web services in this domain introduces real-time requirements. These requirements may vary over time depending on the load of machines or compute nodes. Again, the service quality can only be maintained if changes to the service description can be applied without any difficulty.

- The integration of legacy applications can be burdensome. There is no definite guide on how to split existing software into services. Using one operation for each method may lead to the problem that some of the operations might work on the same variables/resources, such that the services have to share the same state. Encapsulating the state in the operations might eventually lead to one operation for the whole service, which hardly reflects all the functionality in a reasonable way. In this case, many parameters have to be provided, some of which do not have anything to do with the part of the functionality needed. Furthermore, the legacy application could rely on protocols, even proprietary protocols, which can not be described by the service interface.

Fulfilling these requirements allows the support of new types of applications in a SOA based on web services and offers the opportunity for (semi-) automatic client generation. Generally, to describe such requirements and capabilities of web services, different mechanisms can be used. Either new specifications can be created or WS-Policy can be used to specify new policies. WS-Policy [96] is especially useful when it comes to expressing alternative requirements or capabilities of a service, which is the case when different mechanisms or protocols are offered. By exposing a policy, conditions under which a service is provided are exposed.

The policy can be attached to the WSDL description or offered as a separate file. A client may decide by means of a policy whether to invoke a service or not.

WS-Policy does not describe a concrete policy but specifies how to write a concrete policy. A famous example for a WS-Policy is the WS-SecurityPolicy [32] expressing the different security mechanisms supported by a service.

It is reasonable to allow to choose between different protocols for an application, when it comes, for example, to file transfers or streaming, since some of the supported protocols may only be supported natively by a certain programming language (e.g., Java Object Streams) or on a certain operating system (e.g., network protocols). Therefore, WS-Policy is the choice to express these requirements.

By taking a look at a few typical roles usually found in a SOA, it can be shown which problems the actors are involved in. Actors usually execute one or more of the following roles in a service-oriented environment [89]:

1. service developer

2. end users (scientists, "ordinary" Internet users, computer scientists, etc.)

3. service provider (administrator)

4. security manager

5. middleware developer

- The **service developer** is responsible for the application domain coding and is often not a computer scientist, but a domain expert with programming experience, e.g., for engineering, physics, medicine, chemistry, biology, etc. In order to create a service that can be used easily, a service developer often has to design an easy-to-use interface as well as means to transfer large amounts of data. An implementation of these data transfer approaches often does not integrate well into the SOA or induces a huge effort on the service developer or even both. A policy can help to express dependencies on file transfer protocols, how the data transfer is handled and so on. When relying on standard protocols, it may also help to automatically generate and distribute client software, thus alleviating the programming task.

- The **service provider (administrator)** is responsible for setting up the web service engines and Grid middleware as well as all configuration settings. An important part of this role is the management of web and Grid services, especially deployment and undeployment. The deployment of the services also contains the deployment of the policies. Policies help the service provider to describe application dependencies on other protocols and mechanisms. A service provider is able to offer new types of applications as part of the service portfolio, for example, real-time and streaming applications.

- The **end user** actually invokes the service. Thereby, the user should not get in contact with a web service engine or Grid middleware. Technical details like writing client software, manually generating certificate requests, etc. should be hidden from him or her. The invocation is further complicated by the fact that a WSDL description is often not sufficient to describe requirements of a complex service. Often, a user has to guess which security settings are used by a service. File transfers must be handled apart from service invocation, such that the user has to "learn" the file transfer mechanism used and execute it independent of the service invocation possibly with different security settings than the service invocation. Here, again a policy helps to describe security requirements, the protocols used for file transfers, or even the use of streaming protocols allowing for a whole new category of applications to be used as services.

- The **middleware developer** adopts and/or extends the web service engine and Grid middleware according to specific needs. This might, for example, include the adoption of web service specifications not supported by the web service engine or Grid middleware used. A middleware developer must—if necessary—add policy handling capabilities to the middleware used.

- The **security manager** is responsible for the definition and enforcement of security policies[1]. Aspects like data security, authentication and authorization need to be addressed and made consistent with institution standards, current laws, and existing processes. This role is also responsible for monitoring compliance of all systems and services with the policies defined. One of the main difficulties for the security manager is that he has to deal with different interests. On the one hand, there are the users and customers who want easy access to the services. On the other hand, infrastructure and data have to be protected from unauthorized and malicious access. WS-Security policies for the services are defined in collaboration with the service provider.

The situation can even be more complicated if not all participants are members of the same institution. Figure 1.2 shows the different roles and their interactions.

A service provider from institution A may buy software components from an institution B's service development division. Security enhancements for the middleware may even be outsourced to the institution C. Users of institution D or private individuals may use the service.

---

[1]The term policy is here used in the general sense and not in the sense of a WS-Policy.

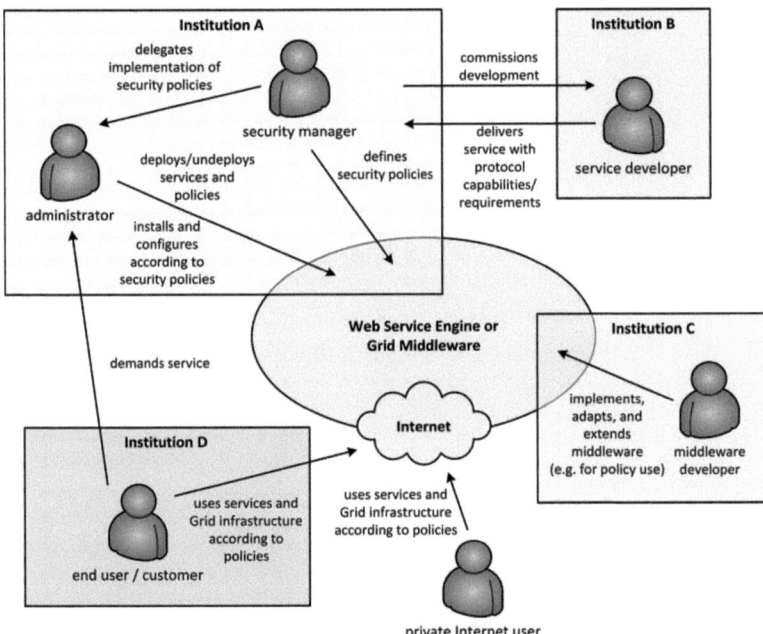

Figure 1.2: Roles in a service-oriented environment relating to services.

1.1 Research Contributions

This thesis aims at increasing the descriptive power of service interfaces by introducing a set of policies that allows the description of a temporal dimension of policies, of file transfers, of clients for services, and of protocols that services depend on in order to express streaming and real-time needs. Being able to describe these requirements and capabilities in the service interface, it is possible to improve efficiency and flexibility of data transmissions, which again offers new opportunities to significantly improve the usability of web and Grid service applications. By using a temporal dimension for policies, it is possible to switch policies depending on the situation of the environment (e.g., load of a computer node, etc.).

This thesis introduces the following contributions.

- **Description of Temporal Dimensions of Services:** Requirements of services cannot be described if they vary over time without the need to manually redeploy the service or the policies. Otherwise, these time-dependent requirements are left undefined resulting in the service being hardly usable at all. To address this problem, a way to model a temporal dimension is needed, so that validity periods for service properties can be defined.

  A temporal policy language is introduced in this thesis to define validity periods for service properties usually expressed by other policies. With these validity periods and an event/action system, it is possible to manage temporal and causal dependencies between different policies.

- **Description of Communication Options for Web Services:** The requirements of web services cannot be described by WSDL when it comes to real-time or streaming requirements, or when special protocols for file transfers or integrating legacy applications are used. Services with such requirements are hard to use without first contacting the service developer or service provider. A means to describe streaming, real-time, and protocol requirements of services is needed. Describing these features is also a first step towards the automatic generation of complex clients for web or Grid services and towards services that rely on efficient streaming or real-time protocols like RTP [86], thus allowing, for example, video-on-demand services.

  To address these requirements, a communication policy describing requirements like streaming and real-time is introduced in this thesis. Special protocol needs can be expressed, so that applications for which the SOAP protocol is unsuited or too inefficient can rely on other, better suitable protocols.

- **Data Handling:** The handling of bulk data with SOAP is very time- and memory-consuming and also inflexible. A user may need—depending on the SOAP engine used—a larger amount of main memory in his or her computer and has to wait a long time until binary data, e.g., a video, or a collection of pictures has been completely transferred. At this point, a more flexible way of handling data in service-oriented environments is needed. This includes—among others—the efficient handling of bulk data as well as "streaming" capabilities, i.e. the repetitive sending of data to a service after its invocation. The data handling capabilities should be hidden in the infrastructure, so that service developers and users do not have to deal with the data handling details. The user should be able to efficiently handle the data in the same step as the service invocation takes place.

To address these data handling needs, the Flex-SwA architecture is presented in this thesis. It allows to efficiently and flexibly handle data transfers outside of the SOAP message by specifying communication patterns and leveraging a reference system, thus reducing time- and memory consumption The Flex-SwA architecture is based on the communication policy that describes the protocols to use for the efficient communication.

- **Familiar Environment for Service Use:** An ordinary Internet user is often not able to invoke a web or Grid service, since programming of a client is normally required. Even if clients exist, they are often hard to use. The user has to install a specific middleware, know about environment variables and program libraries to use, etc. To help a user to actually invoke a service, two steps are required. First, to actually use web or Grid services, a prospective user should be able to search for available services. In the web service area, a Web Service Crawler engine [8], which searches the Web for available web services, exists. Since most Grids are built nation-wide and Grid service WSDLs are normally not found on the World Wide Web, a Grid service search engine is needed knowing different locations and Grid nodes to search for services as well as a suitable retrieval function. Second, the user needs means to invoke a service without having to set up a Grid middleware or web service engine and without programming client software himself or herself.

  As a familiar environment for most users, a Web and Grid Service Browser is presented in this thesis. A graphical user interface is generated from the WSDL description of a service, so that the user can actually invoke a service without any programming experience and without knowing which middleware is used. Even data transfers can be integrated, if services support the Flex-SwA architecture and the data transfers are described by the communication policy, such that a user does not need to transfer large data sets in advance.

- **End User Involvement:** Sometimes, applications do not directly suit the needs of an application user. Therefore, it is a good idea to involve the

1.1. Research Contributions

end user in the application design. A mechanism for this are mashups. They often support a common set of APIs, sometimes even RESTful web services, but totally lack the connection to web services based on SOAP and the Grid. It should be possible to leverage existing Grid services and resources to build value-added web mashups.

A mashup editor that allows end users to develop simple Grid applications combined with popular web applications is introduced in this thesis. Again, data handling capabilities of the Flex-SwA architecture can be used if described by a communication policy.

Parts of the research presented in this thesis are used in the German D-Grid Initiative [81] (In-Grid and F&L-Grid project) and in the research center "Media Upheavals" (SFB/FK615) located at the Universities of Siegen and Marburg and funded by the German Research Foundation (Deutsche Forschungsgemeinschaft, DFG). The temporal policy language has been part of an IBM Real-time Innovation Award (2008) winning proposal. As part of the research conducted in this thesis, the following papers have been published:

1. M. Mathes, S. Heinzl, T. Friese, B. Freisleben: *Enabling Post-Invocation Parameter Transmission in Service-Oriented Environments*, Proc. of the Int'l Conf. on Networking and Services, pp. 55-60, IEEE Press, 2006

2. S. Heinzl, M. Mathes, T. Friese, M. Smith, B. Freisleben: *Flex-SwA: Flexible Exchange of Binary Data Based on SOAP Messages with Attachments*, Proc. of the IEEE Int'l Conf. on Web Services, pp. 3-10, IEEE Press, 2006

3. T. Dörnemann, S. Heinzl, K. Dörnemann, M. Mathes, M. Smith, B. Freisleben: *Secure Grid Service Engineering for Industrial Optimization*, Proc. of the 7th Int'l Conf. on Optimization: Techniques and Applications (ICOTA), pp. 371-372, 2007

4. S. Heinzl, M. Mathes, B. Freisleben: *A Web Service Communication Policy for Describing Non-Standard Application Requirements*, Proc. of the IEEE/IPSJ Symposium on Applications and the Internet (Saint), pp. 40-47, IEEE Press, 2008

5. M. Mathes, S. Heinzl, B. Freisleben: *WS-TemporalPolicy: A WS-Policy Extension for Describing Service Properties with Time Constraints*, Proc. of the 1st IEEE Int'l Workshop On Real-Time Service-Oriented Architecture and Applications (RTSOAA) of the 32nd IEEE Computer Software and Applications Conference (COMPSAC), pp. 1180-1186, IEEE Press, 2008

6. R. Schwarzkopf, M. Mathes, S. Heinzl, B. Freisleben, H. Dohmann: *Java RMI versus .NET Remoting - Architectural Comparison and Performance*

Evaluation, Proc. of the 7th Int'l Conf. on Networking (ICN), pp. 398-407, IEEE Press, 2008

7. M. Mathes, R. Schwarzkopf, T. Dörnemann, S. Heinzl, B. Freisleben: *Orchestration of Time-Constrained BPEL4WS Workflows,* Proc. of the 13th IEEE Int'l Conf. on Emerging Technologies and Factory Automation (ETFA), pp. 1-4, IEEE Press, 2008

8. M. Mathes, S. Heinzl, B. Freisleben: *Towards a Time-Constrained Web Service Infrastructure for Industrial Automation,* Proc. of the 13th IEEE Int'l Conf. on Emerging Technologies and Factory Automation (ETFA), pp. 846-853, IEEE Press, 2008

9. D. Seiler, S. Heinzl, E. Juhnke, R. Ewerth, M. Grauer, B. Freisleben: *Efficient Data Transmission in Service Workflows for Distributed Video Content Analysis,* Proc. of the 6th Int'l Conf. on Advances in Mobile Computing and Multimedia (MoMM), pp. 7-14, ACM and OCG Book Series, 2008

10. S. Heinzl, M. Mathes, B. Freisleben: *The Grid Browser: Improving Usability in Service-Oriented Grids by Automatically Generating Clients and Handling Data Transfers,* Proc. of the 4th IEEE Int'l Conf. on e-Science, pp. 269-276, IEEE Press, 2008

11. M. Mathes, C. Stoidner, S. Heinzl, B. Freisleben: *SOAP4PLC: Web Services for Programmable Logic Controllers,* Proc. of the 7th Euromicro Int'l Conf. on Parallel, Distributed, and Network-Based Processing (Euromicro PDP), pp. 210-219, IEEE Press, 2009

12. M. Mathes, S. Heinzl, B. Freisleben: *Towards a Generic Backup and Recovery Infrastructure for the D-Grid Initiative,* 16. ITG/GI Fachtagung - Kommunikation in Verteilten Systemen (KiVS), pp. 229-240, Springer-Verlag, 2009

13. M. Mathes, S. Heinzl, R. Schwarzkopf, B. Freisleben: *F&L-Grid: Eine generische Backup und Recovery Infrastruktur für das D-Grid,* Lecture Notes in Informatics, pp. (accepted for publication), Gesellschaft für Informatik (GI), 2009

14. M. Mathes, R. Schwarzkopf, T. Dörnemann, S. Heinzl, B. Freisleben: *Composition of Time-Constrained BPEL4WS Workflows using the TiCS Modeler,* Proc. of the 13th IFAC Symposium on Information Control Problems in Manufacturing, pp. (accepted for publication), 2009

15. S. Heinzl, D. Seiler, E. Juhnke, T. Stadelmann, R. Ewerth, M. Grauer, B. Freisleben: *A Scalable Service-Oriented Architecture for Multimedia Analysis, Synthesis, and Consumption,* Int'l J. of Web and Grid Services, pp. (accepted for publication), Inderscience Publishers, 2009

16. S. Heinzl, M. Mathes, T. Stadelmann, D. Seiler, M. Diegelmann, H. Dohmann, B. Freisleben: *The Web Service Browser: Automatic Client Generation and Efficient Data Transfer for Web Services,* Proc. of the 7th IEEE Int'l Conf. on Web Services (ICWS), pp. (accepted for publication), IEEE Press, 2009

1.2 Organization of the Thesis

This thesis is organized into 11 chapters.

- Chapter 2 presents an overview of the web service policies introduced and the components built upon these policies.

- Chapter 3 presents a temporal policy for web services to add a temporal dimension to the requirement descriptions done by WS-Policies.

- Chapter 4 presents a communication policy for web services to describe non-standard application requirements.

- Chapter 5 presents the Flex-SwA architecture for flexible and efficient data handling in service-oriented environments.

- Chapter 6 presents the Web and Grid Service Browser to improve usability of web and Grid services.

- Chapter 7 shows a mashup editor that leverages Grid resources and combines popular web applications with web and Grid services.

- Chapter 8 presents the implementation of the components introduced in this thesis.

- Chapter 9 presents an evaluation of the introduced components.

- Chapter 10 presents related work to the different working areas.

- Chapter 11 concludes this thesis with a summary and an outlook on future work.

2
Policies for Web Services

2.1 Introduction

This chapter provides an overview of how web services can be improved in the areas of

- Description of Temporal Dimensions
- Description of Communication Options
- Flexible and Efficient Data Handling
- Simple Service Use
- Leveraging Grid resources for end user development.

Different policies have been designed to allow the definition of validity periods, events and actions, the use of protocols suited for real-time, streaming, and file transfers, and integration of legacy applications based on standard or proprietary protocols. Figure 2.1 shows the policies and the components built upon them.

A temporal policy allows the definition of validity periods of WS-Policies as well as the definition of events and actions taking place when events are triggered. The validity periods may, for example, specify how long certain communication protocols (allowing a service to achieve streaming or meet real-time requirements), can be used with a certain service. The validity periods make sense when protocol versions are updated or when the communication protocols depend on the load of the service. Since such communication protocol needs can not be expressed with standard WSDL or already existing policies, WS-CommunicationPolicy is introduced in this thesis for this purpose. With a communication policy, it is possible for a service to describe the protocols it needs

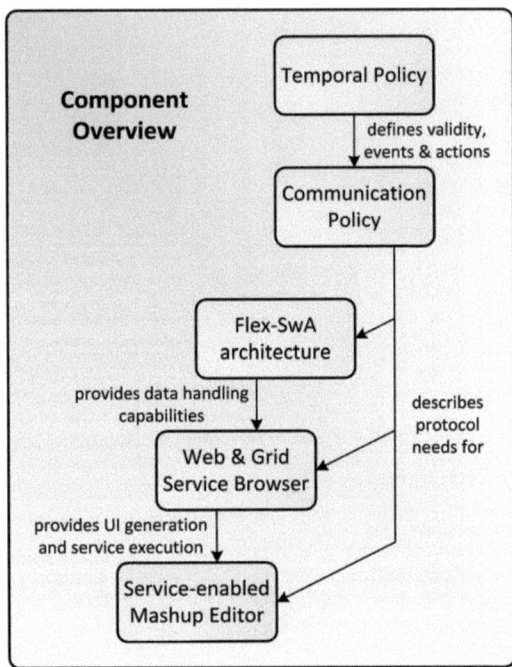

Figure 2.1: Component overview.

to fulfill, for example, real-time requirements. With Flex-SwA, an architecture is introduced that provides data handling capabilities to services, such that data transfers can be handled flexibly and efficiently, data streaming is possible, and messages can be sent repetitively to services with a specified message encoding. With the descriptive power of the communication policy and the Flex-SwA architecture, it is possible to develop a new way to easily invoke web and Grid services: a Web and Grid Services Browser. The Web and Grid Services Browser—in contrast to a portal—generates the user interface automatically and thus relieves the service developer from developing a client and a portlet and the service provider from maintaining the portal. Furthermore, the user can be involved in creating new applications based on web and Grid services combined with popular services in the Web. The user interface generation and service invocation capabilities of the Web and Grid Service Browser are then used for a Service-enabled Mashup Editor. The Mashup Editor combines popular web applications with web and Grid services, for example, face detection in videos or images from the multimedia area.

2.2 Temporal Policy: Description of Temporal Dimensions

Whereas the Web Service Description Language (WSDL) [29] is used to describe the *functional properties* of a web service (operations offered, messages used for invocation, etc.), many web services have additional *non-functional properties*, such as time constraints, quality of service parameters, and security properties. These non-functional properties are often dynamic, e.g., time constraints like the average and worst-case execution time that may vary over time depending on the current workload. Although there are several standards for describing non-functional properties of web services, it has up to now been challenging for a web service developer to describe non-functional properties with dynamic characteristics.

A temporal policy allows to add a validity period to dynamic properties of web services and WS-Policies. Events and actions can be used to handle temporal dependencies between different policies.

2.3 Communication Policy: Description of Communication Options

The idea of a SOA comprises that a SOA is capable of describing all the interfaces of the services it consists of. In SOAs based on web services, the service descriptions are often not sufficient to, for example, generate clients, since it is not possible to directly express protocol requirements of services. For example, applications requiring data streaming, time constraints (real-time), transfer of large files, or legacy applications with complex message exchange patterns cannot be described with WSDL. Such applications tend to rely on other protocols especially suited to fulfill these requirements. To integrate such applications into a SOA, the requirements must be described by the service. This can be done by the communication policy introduced in this thesis. The communication policy is based on WS-Policy and extends the descriptive power of WSDL. Thus, different protocols that can be used to communicate with a service can be exposed.

The idea of the communication policy is that a service is capable of describing its means of communication in addition to the WSDL description. By providing the necessary protocol information, a web service client is able to use other protocols to communicate with a service (for example, real-time protocols) and leverage efficient binary file transfer protocols. With well-known protocol descriptions, a (semi-)automatic generation of client software is possible or the location of suitable clients and their requirements can be described.

2.4 Flex-SwA: Architecture for Data Handling

SOAP is commonly used to invoke web or Grid services. Parameters for the target operation are usually embedded in the SOAP message as long as these parameters are primitive ones like integers, strings, or floating point numbers. Problems occur when larger amounts of binary data have to be transferred because of the time taken by the encoding, the inflation of the amount of data due to the encoding, and the memory consumption when a whole SOAP message part has to be handled.

Also, when small messages have to be sent repetitively, the SOAP envelope induces a huge overhead compared to the size of the message payload.

To avoid these disadvantages, an architecture for flexibly handling data in service-oriented environments called *Flex-SwA* is presented in this thesis. Being based on references pointing to data locations, it allows message forwarding without additional communication cost as well as demand-driven evaluation and transmission of binary data. Additionally, Flex-SwA offers several communication patterns—allowing the service developer to focus on service development instead of data transmission—and post-invocation parameter transmission (PIPT)—empowering a developer to invoke a service and subsequently send parameters to it after its invocation. For the transfer of large amounts of data and the repetitive sending of data, suitable protocols that are described in a communication policy can be chosen.

2.5 Web and Grid Service Browser: Familiar Environment for Service Use

The complexity of Grid service development is very high. For each service, a client program has to be developed. If a service provider does not offer a client, it is impossible for users without programming knowledge to use the services. Large data transfers are a problem as well. If done via SOAP, data transmission and service invocation is performed in a single step, but the processing of SOAP messages is very memory- and time-consuming. When done in two steps, data and sometimes executables are moved to the service location and then the service is invoked. The service invocation is started after the data has arrived at the service location, such that the user has to wait with the service invocation for a non-negligible amount of time. Furthermore, the user must know where the data has to be sent to and how to achieve this. Here, the communication policy helps with the description and the Flex-SwA implementation with a user-friendly transfer of the data.

A Web and Grid Service Browser is introduced in this thesis as a familiar environment for accessing web or Grid services. When browsing to a WSDL description of a service, a user experiences a generated graphical frontend, via which it is possible to easily invoke the service. From the user's view, data transfers are handled in a single step. In the background, the Flex-SwA implementation is used to efficiently transmit the data in the same step as the service invocation takes place. Thus, the user is able to use web and Grid services with significantly less effort. Furthermore, there is no need for the service developer to develop a graphical user interface for the service user anymore, since Grid service clients are automatically generated on the fly.

2.6 Web and Grid Service-enabled Mashup Editor

It may be very attractive for end users to leverage high performance computing resources, for example, in the multimedia area. It could, for example, be interesting to identify an actor in a video clip or generate a preview of a video by showing one picture of each shot of a video. But these tasks are so computationally intensive that, for example, Grid or Cloud resources are needed to achieve a reasonable runtime behaviour. Again, the major obstacle for end users is that such services and applications are hard to use without proper programming skills.

To utilize high performance resources in (self-defined) applications, a mashup editor can be used, since the main focus of mashups is simplicity, ease of use, and simple access. It is even possible to integrate web and Grid services into popular web applications by using a communication policy to describe the protocols and implementing the communication via Flex-SwA.

2.7 Summary

This section gave an overview of how policies contribute to solve several shortcomings of SOAs based on web or Grid services. By describing temporal aspects and protocols a service relies on, it is possible to build flexible and efficient data transfers, enable streaming and real-time applications as services, automatically generate web/Grid service clients allowing a user to easily invoke a service, and to combine web and Grid services with popular web applications to mashups while leveraging high performance computing resources.

3

Describing Temporal Dimensions of Policies

3.1 Introduction

In this chapter, *WS-TemporalPolicy*, a policy language for extending web service policies [96] by temporal aspects is introduced (Figure 3.1). A Temporal Policy Runtime Environment consisting of different components manages dependencies between different temporal policies. A state model defines the states which a policy can be in. *Parts of this chapter have been published in [72]*.

Currently, web services are the de facto standard for realizing service-oriented architectures (SOAs). The Web Service Description Language (WSDL) [28] is used to describe the interface of a web service, i.e. the operations offered and the messages necessary to invoke an operation. Hence, a WSDL document is used to describe the *functional* properties of a service, which normally do not vary over the time.

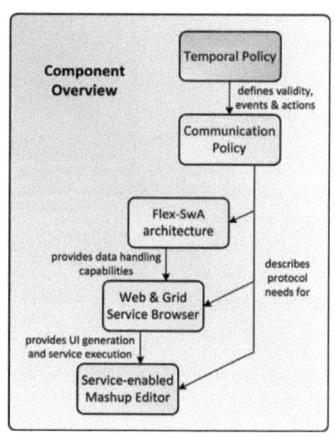

Figure 3.1: Overview: Temporal Policy.

In addition to the functional properties, many web services have *non-functional* properties, such as quality of service (QoS) or security properties. These non-functional properties are often dynamic—an example is a QoS property like the response time of a service, which may vary over time depending on the current workload. Although there are several standards for describing different non-functional properties of web services, it is not possible for a service developer to describe temporal non-functional properties. WS-TemporalPolicy is a novel approach that enables the description of such properties.

3.2 The Need for Dynamic Properties

There are several web service specifications that provide a rich, well-defined set of features for loosely-coupled, standardized, service-based applications. These specifications are highly extensible to cover requirements the authors of the specifications could not anticipate. In particular, WS-Policy allows the description of the behavior of a service by specifying several properties, which can be associated with the service's WSDL description.

Up to now, many service properties can be described, for example,

(1) port type, operations, messages, message parts and bindings by WSDL,

(2) QoS parameters by a QoS policy [43],

(3) security configurations by a security policy [32],

(4) service addressing by an addressing policy [49], and

(5) semantics of a service by ontologies [31].

Using these descriptions, it is possible to define a wide range of service properties. New policies can be defined for specific domain needs if these have not been addressed yet. All of these properties have one thing in common: they are *static* properties. When the service is defined, it is assumed that these properties will never change. However, this does not hold, for example, for QoS parameters, where the workload of the infrastructure influences the behavior of the services. Therefore, there is a need to describe *dynamic* properties of a service. Up to now, these properties can only be provided in the functional layer of the service as a service operation. However, conceptually, monitoring data about a service should be provided as part of the service's metadata, i.e. WSDL description and policies. To describe these dynamic properties, a new policy type—a temporal policy called *WS-TemporalPolicy*— is introduced and the *Temporal Policy Runtime Environment* allowing the management of these policies is presented.

3.3 Temporal Policies

This section explains how temporal policies are defined and can be used to describe dynamic properties. For this purpose, WS-Policy is presented here briefly.

3.3. Temporal Policies 23

Furthermore, it is shown how WS-Policy can be used in combination with a WS-TemporalPolicy.

3.3.1 WS-Policy

The web service policy (WS-Policy) [96] language enables the definition of policies for web services. A policy is used to describe the properties, i.e. capabilities and requirements, of a service and is attached either to the WSDL document or exposed as a separate file. Based on the properties defined in a WS-Policy, a potential service requestor can decide whether this service satisfies its requirements. With WS-Policy, only static properties can be defined.

Within a WS-Policy, an `ExactlyOne` element can be used to define a set of alternatives from which exactly one can be chosen by the service requestor. To define a list of mandatory properties, the `All` element can be used. An arbitrary nesting of `ExactlyOne` and `All` elements is possible to describe complex structures of alternative and mandatory properties. Listings 3.1 and 3.2 show the use of the `ExactlyOne` and `All` element (namespaces are omitted for simplicity).

```
<Policy Name="http://fb12.de/sampleWSPolicy1">
  <ExactlyOne>
    <!-- alternative 1 -->
    <!-- ... -->
    <!-- alternative n -->
  </ExactlyOne>
</Policy>
```

Listing 3.1: Example of a WS-Policy using `ExactlyOne`.

```
<Policy Name="http://fb12.de/sampleWSPolicy2">
  <All>
    <!-- mandatory property 1 -->
    <!-- ... -->
    <!-- mandatory property n -->
  </All>
</Policy>
```

Listing 3.2: Example of a WS-Policy using `All`.

3.3.2 Temporal Policy Schema

The proposed temporal policy defines the validity period of a WS-Policy. This can be done by using the attributes `expires`, `startTime` and `endTime`, or `duration`. The `expires` attribute defines how long a policy is valid, whereas the `startTime` and `endTime` attributes define a time slot during which the policy is valid. The `duration` attribute is used to specify a relative amount of time for the validity of the policy. Every temporal policy has a `name` attribute that defines the unique name of this policy and an optional `keywords` attribute that eases the retrieval of a temporal policy from a temporal policy repository (see section 3.4). The schema of a temporal policy is defined via XML Schema [23], as shown in Listings 3.3 and 3.4.

```
<xs:schema
 targetNamespace="http://fb12.de/2007/09/temporalpolicy"
 xmlns:xs="http://www.w3.org/2001/XMLSchema"
 xmlns="http://fb12.de/2007/09/temporalpolicy"
 elementFormDefault="qualified">

<xs:complexType name="actionType">
 <xs:sequence>
  <xs:element name="activate"
  minOccurs="0" maxOccurs="unbounded">
   <xs:complexType>
    <xs:attribute name="ref" type="xs:anyURI" use="required"/>
   </xs:complexType>
  </xs:element>
  <xs:element name="renew"
  minOccurs="0" maxOccurs="unbounded">
   <xs:complexType>
    <xs:choice>
     <xs:element name="expires" type="xs:dateTime"/>
     <xs:sequence>
      <xs:element name="startTime" type="xs:dateTime"/>
      <xs:element name="endTime" type="xs:dateTime"/>
     </xs:sequence>
     <xs:element name="duration" type="xs:duration"/>
    </xs:choice>
    <xs:attribute name="ref" type="xs:anyURI" use="required"/>
   </xs:complexType>
  </xs:element>
  <xs:element name="deactivate"
  minOccurs="0" maxOccurs="unbounded">
   <xs:complexType>
    <xs:attribute name="ref" type="xs:anyURI" use="required"/>
   </xs:complexType>
  </xs:element>
 </xs:sequence>
</xs:complexType>
```

Listing 3.3: XML schema for a temporal policy (part I).

First, a `complexType` named `actionType` is defined. An `actionType` consists of three optional elements each of which may appear several times. The elements

3.3. Temporal Policies

are **activate**, **renew**, and **deactivate**. Each element contains an attribute **ref** which references the policy to activate, renew, or deactivate. The **renew** element additionally either contains an **expires** element, the elements **startTime** and **endTime** (represented by the **dateTime** type of XML Schema), or the **duration** element (represented by the XML Schema's **duration** type).

```
<xs:element name="temporalPolicy">
 <xs:complexType>
  <!-- child elements of a temporal policy -->
   <xs:sequence>
    <xs:choice>
     <xs:element name="expires" type="xs:dateTime"/>
     <xs:sequence>
      <xs:element name="startTime" type="xs:dateTime"/>
      <xs:element name="endTime" type="xs:dateTime"/>
     </xs:sequence>
     <xs:element name="duration" type="xs:duration"/>
    </xs:choice>
    <xs:element name="onActivation" type="actionType"
      minOccurs="0" maxOccurs="1"/>
    <xs:element name="onRenewal" type="actionType"
      minOccurs="0" maxOccurs="1"/>
    <xs:element name="onExpiration" type="actionType"
      minOccurs="0" maxOccurs="1"/>
    <xs:element name="onDeactivation" type="actionType"
      minOccurs="0" maxOccurs="1"/>
   </xs:sequence>
   <!-- attributes of a temporal policy -->
   <xs:attribute name="name" type="xs:anyURI" use="required"/>
   <xs:attribute name="keywords" type="xs:string"/>
  </xs:complexType>
 </xs:element>
</xs:schema>
```
Listing 3.4: XML schema for a temporal policy (part II).

The second part of the Temporal Policy schema describes the root element, the **temporalPolicy** element of a temporal policy. The **temporalPolicy** element contains—like the renew element—, either an **expires** element, **startTime** and **endTime**, or a **duration** element. Furthermore, it may contain several **actionType** elements: **onActivation**, **onRenewal**, **onExpiration**, **onDeactivation**. Finally, a temporal policy has the following attributes: **name** and **keywords**. The **name** attribute represents the name for the policy and is required. The **keywords** attribute is of type string and lists several keywords used for the retrieval of policies.

3.3.3 Temporal Policy Referencing WS-Policies

Listing 3.5 shows a temporal policy that is valid until January 1st, 2012 and defines the validity period for a WS-Policy named http://fb12.de/wsPolicy1 by using the renew action when activated (see Tables 3.1 and 3.2) and the expires element. Listing 3.6 shows a temporal policy defining the validity period for a WS-Policy named http://fb12.de/wsPolicy2 using the elements startTime and endTime. Additionally, the first policy defines three keywords to easily retrieve this policy from a temporal policy repository.

```
<temporalPolicy xmlns="http://fb12.de/2007/09/temporalpolicy"
  name="http://fb12.de/sampleTemporalPolicy1"
  keywords="keyword1 keyword2 keyword3">
  <expires>2012-01-01T00:00:00</expires>
  <onActivation>
    <renew ref="http://fb12.de/wsPolicy1">
      <expires>2009-07-01T00:00:00</expires>
    </renew>
  </onActivation>
</temporalPolicy>
```

Listing 3.5: Example of a temporal policy using the expires element.

```
<temporalPolicy xmlns="http://fb12.de/2007/09/temporalpolicy"
  name="http://fb12.de/sampleTemporalPolicy2">
  <expires>2012-01-01T00:00:00</expires>
  <onActivation>
    <renew ref="http://fb12.de/wsPolicy2">
      <startTime>2009-07-01T00:00:00</startTime>
      <endTime>2010-01-01T00:00:00</endTime>
    </renew>
  </onActivation>
</temporalPolicy>
```

Listing 3.6: Example of a temporal policy using the startTime and endTime elements.

3.3.4 Actions and Event Handlers

It is possible to activate/renew/deactivate a temporal policy depending on another temporal policy using *actions* and *event handlers*, e.g., a temporal policy is activated when another temporal policy is deactivated or vice versa. Dependencies between temporal policies are described by the definition of event handler elements and corresponding action elements. Table 3.1 gives an overview of possible events handlers, whereas table 3.2 gives an overview of possible actions.

3.3. Temporal Policies

Table 3.1: Overview of event handlers in temporal policies.

Event	Description
onActivation	The onActivation event occurs when a temporal policy is activated. The referenced policies are attached to the WSDL description of a service.
onExpiration	The onExpiration event occurs when the validity period of a policy expires.
onRenewal	The onRenewal event occurs if a temporal policy is renewed, i.e. its validity period is modified.
onDeactivation	This event occurs when a temporal policy is deactivated. The referenced policies are detached from the WSDL description of a service.

Table 3.2: Overview of actions in temporal policies.

Action	Description
activate	A policy is activated, i.e. it is attached to the WSDL description of a service or in case of a temporal policy it issues its own actions.
renew	The validity period of a policy is modified.
deactivate	A policy is removed from the WSDL description of a service or in case of a temporal policy does not execute further actions or trigger events.

28 Describing Temporal Dimensions of Policies

The described event handler/action elements enable the definition of complex temporal policy dependencies, which can be visualized via a dependency tree. An example tree is shown in Figure 3.2 containing five temporal policies and five WS-Policies. The event handlers are written in italics, whereas the corresponding actions are written in bold.

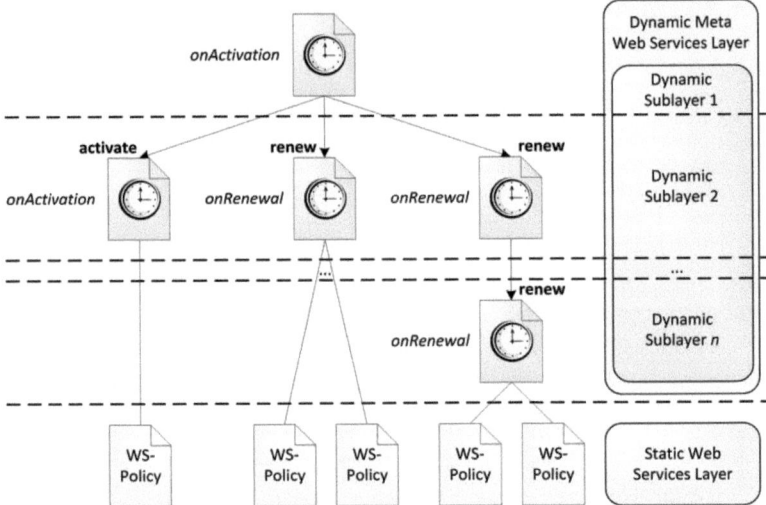

Figure 3.2: Dependency tree for several WS-TemporalPolicies and WS-Policies.

As shown in the dependency tree, the use of WS-TemporalPolicy induces several logical layers ranging from static to dynamic with regard to the validity period. The static web services layer includes the operations. Above the web services layer, the dynamic meta web services layer is located; it can be divided into n sublayers. Each sublayer handles a different temporal dimension. At the top layer, there might be a temporal policy that defines its (long-lasting) validity period (e.g., by referencing itself) and handles other temporal policies. These policies again could manage other policies, which are, for example, valid for months, weeks, days and so on. In this way, different layers can be built to enable a fine-grained (hierarchical) management of the validity of policies.

The use of event handlers and actions is exemplified in Listing 3.7. The defined sampleTemporalPolicy3 does not influence a concrete WS-Policy (though this would be possible as well), but the temporal policies sampleTemporalPolicy1 and sampleTemporalPolicy2. It defines that on its activation the sampleTemporalPolicy1 is also activated, whereas the sampleTemporalPolicy2 is de-

3.4. The Temporal Policy Runtime Environment

activated. On its deactivation, the `sampleTemporalPolicy1` is also deactivated, whereas the `sampleTemporalPolicy2` is activated. Furthermore, a modification of the validity period of this temporal policy results in a modification of the validity period of `sampleTemporalPolicy1` and `sampleTemporalPolicy2`.

```
<temporalPolicy xmlns="http://fb12.de/2007/09/temporalpolicy"
  name="http://fb12.de/sampleTemporalPolicy3">
  <expires>2012-01-01T00:00:00</expires>
  <onActivation>
    <activate ref="http://fb12.de/sampleTemporalPolicy1"/>
    <deactivate ref="http://fb12.de/sampleTemporalPolicy2"/>
  </onActivation>
  <onRenewal>
    <renew ref="http://fb12.de/sampleTemporalPolicy1">
      <expires>2010-07-01T00:00:00</expires>
    </renew>
    <renew ref="http://fb12.de/sampleTemporalPolicy2">
      <startTime>2010-07-01T00:00:00</startTime>
      <endTime>2010-12-01T00:00:00</endTime>
    </renew>
  </onRenewal>
  <onDeactivation>
    <activate ref="http://fb12.de/sampleTemporalPolicy2"/>
    <deactivate ref="http://fb12.de/sampleTemporalPolicy1"/>
  </onDeactivation>
</temporalPolicy>
```
Listing 3.7: Example of a temporal policy that affects other temporal policies.

3.4 The Temporal Policy Runtime Environment

The *Temporal Policy Runtime Environment* is a set of functional components enabling the creation, validation, storage, discovery, and deployment of temporal policies. Figure 3.3 shows these components and their interactions to attach a temporal policy to a web service. Figure 3.4 shows the states a policy can be in.

First of all, a temporal policy is a simple XML document. Since real-world applications may produce a multiplicity of temporal policies that have to be organized and eventually saved, a *repository* is necessary to organize the policies (for example in a database or as flat files). The *repository manager* enables easy storing of temporal policies in and retrieval of temporal policies from the repository. It should be possible to retrieve a temporal policy using its identifier or several keywords. To empower the user to easily define and validate a new temporal policy, the Temporal Policy Runtime Environment contains a *generator* and *validator* component. Both components are interconnected to enable policy validation during the creation process. The validator component especially checks

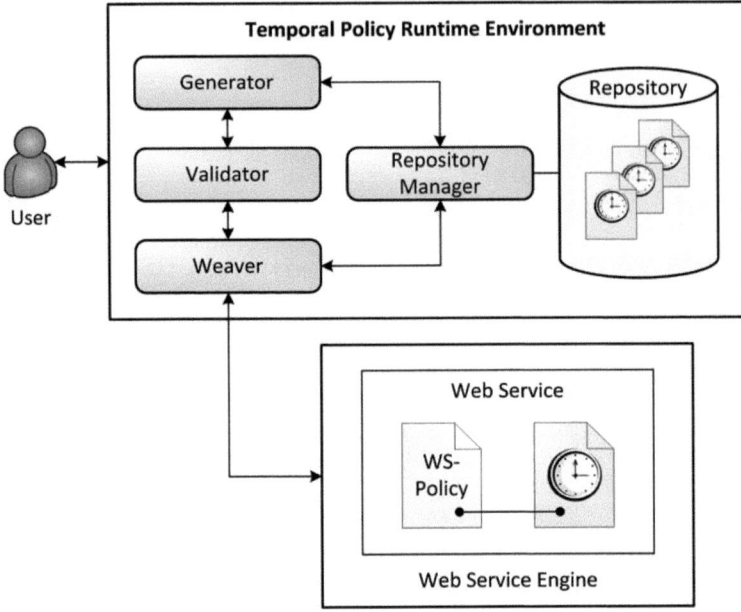

Figure 3.3: Functional components of the temporal policy runtime environment.

that a new temporal policy does not collide with an existing already deployed temporal policy. To attach a policy to the WSDL description of a web service—based on a temporal policy—a specialized *weaver* is used. The weaver weaves a valid policy to a specific extension point in the WSDL description.

A policy is always in one of the following states: *created*, *activated*, or *deactivated*. When the Temporal Policy Runtime Environment is started, all temporal policies and WS-Policies are in the state *created*. Every policy, whose start time lies in the past or a policy for which an expiration time or a duration is set, immediately changes its state to *activated*. When a policy's end time occurs, a policy expires, or a policy's duration is over, then the policy changes its state from *activated* to *deactivated*. It is also possible to change a policy's state from *activated* to *deactivated* by issuing a **deactivate** action. From the **deactivated** state a policy can either change to the *activated* state by being target of an **activate** action or to the *created* state by being target of a **renew** action. Then, the policy either remains in the *created* state till its start time occurs or is immediately *activated* when the start time is already in the past or the duration or expires element is specified.

3.5. Exposing Validity Dates to the Service User

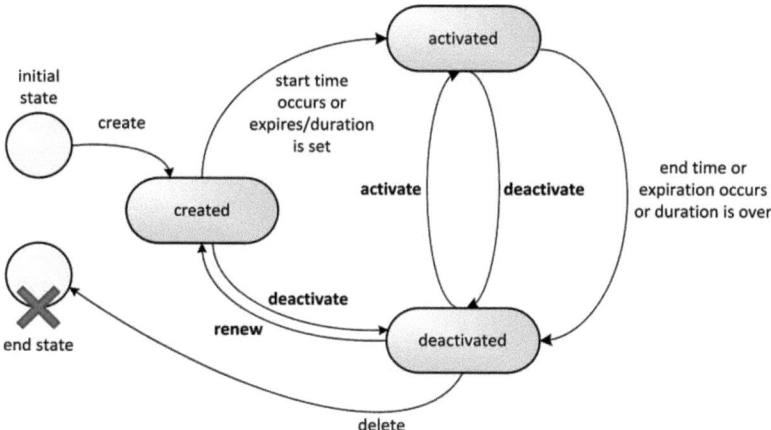

Figure 3.4: States of a policy.

3.5 Exposing Validity Dates to the Service User

With a more fine-grained weaving and a finer property picking (e.g., via XPath), it is possible to expose absolute validity dates to the service user. The validity date can be added as an additional attribute taken from the temporal policy namespace. Listing 3.8 shows a pricing policy for a compute service with the valid attribute from the temporal policy namespace.

```
<wsp:Policy Name="http://example.com/pricingPolicyDay"
  xmlns:wsp="http://www.w3.org/ns/ws-policy"
  xmlns:tp="http://fb12.de/2007/09/temporalpolicy">
  <wsp:ExactlyOne>
    <computeParameters processors="1" primaryMemory="2GB"
      costsPerHour="0.18EUR" costsPerGBDataTransfer="0.12EUR"
      tp:valid="2010-07-01Z"/>
    ...
  </wsp:ExactlyOne>
</wsp:Policy>
```

Listing 3.8: Example of a policy that exposes a validity date.

The only problem that occurs when validity dates are exposed to service users is that the temporal policies determining the validity period for the policies must not be deactivated before the end of the policy's validity period. Otherwise, a policy with a guaranteed validity date is removed from the service although a service user might rely on the offered validity date.

3.6 Summary

This chapter has identified the need for a temporal dimension for dynamic service properties. To describe the temporal dimension, a temporal policy language has been introduced as well as a Temporal Policy Runtime Environment and a state model for the policies. Temporal policies can be used to influence other temporal policies and WS-Policies by defining validity periods for them, issuing actions, and reacting to incoming events. With the action/event handler mechanism, a dependency tree for policies can be defined. With a fine-grained weaving process, it is possible to expose validity dates to service users.

4

Defining Communication Options for Web Services

4.1 Introduction

In this chapter, the need for describing communication options for web and Grid services is derived and WS-Communication Policy introduced (Figure 4.1) to provide the needed descriptive means. *Parts of this chapter have been published in [53].*

One of the major strengths of a SOA is its capability to describe all the interfaces of the services it consists of. It is possible to generate client software capable of invoking a service, just from the service's interface description. However, when using the popular web service technology to implement a SOA, the service descriptions are not sufficient. Several limitations have not yet been addressed by web service specifications. For example, requirements of data streaming or real-time applications, of applications depending on the transfer of large files, and requirements of legacy applications with complex message exchange patterns cannot be described with WSDL. Services with such requirements tend to rely on other protocols especially suited to fulfill these requirements. To

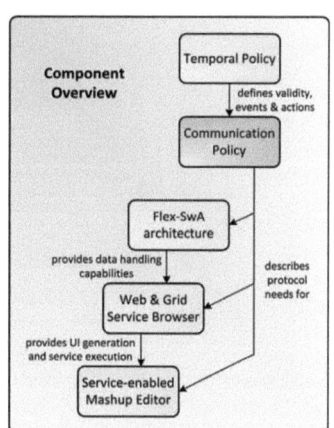

Figure 4.1: Overview: Communication Policy.

use such a protocol in a web service based SOA, it must either be implemented over SOAP or the application must be wrapped by a web service, in which case the needed protocol is not part of the service description.

When new services are written, these are typically designed as independent components and can thus be easily used in a SOA whereas legacy applications are divided into functional components each wrapped by a web service. A problem occurs when the service or the legacy application includes the sending of many messages or when the messages have to be received and processed in a predefined time. Then, either many web services have to be used or a non-negligible overhead is added by implementing existing protocols over SOAP (especially when the messages are short), or both.

Finding a way to describe these requirements promises automatic client generation and thus no need for the user to write a client on its own, or at least a (semi-)automatic installation of the software. Also, a service provider is able to offer new types of applications as part of his/her SOA. The installation process for the user is eased. Up to now, there have been three common solutions to this problem.

The first solution is to turn down the advantages of web services and simply develop the application with a suitable middleware technology and suitable protocols. Figure 4.2 shows the steps a customer needs to take to use such a non-integrated application.

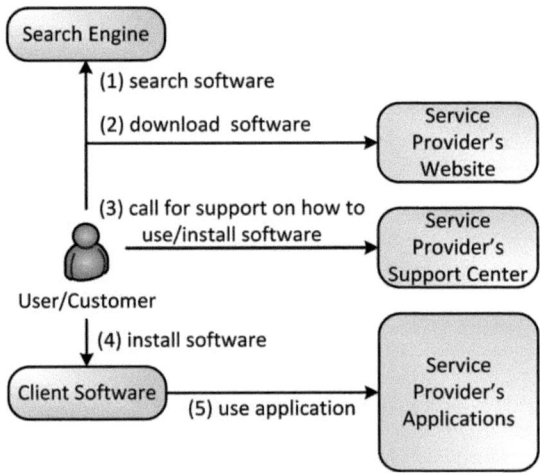

Figure 4.2: Application without SOA integration.

(1) First, the user searches the required software via a search engine.

4.1. Introduction

(2) When the software has been found, the user downloads it from the service provider's website or from the website of an external provider,

(3) asks for support on how to use/install it at the service provider's support center (optionally), and

(4) installs the software.

(5) The application can then be used.

The installed client software is capable of interacting with the application offered by the provider. The customer needs to know where to obtain the software from and how to install and use it. In this architecture, no feature that constitutes a SOA is used. If the provider uses a SOA, the application runs completely independent of it.

The second solution (shown in Figure 4.3) is to write a web service wrapper for the application and then use the protocols of the application in the background.

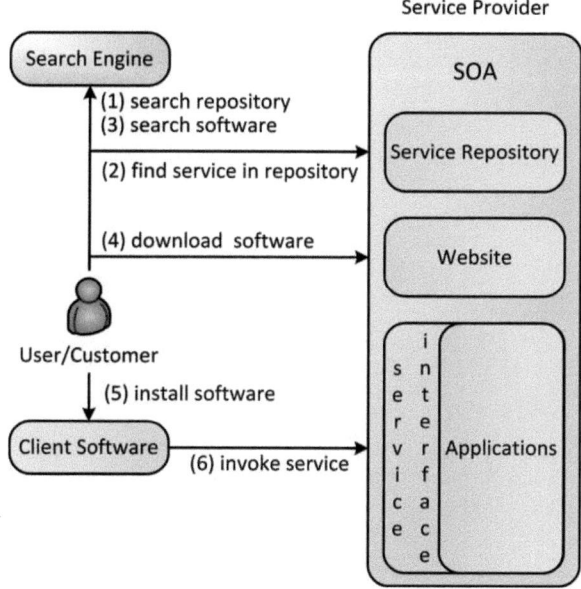

Figure 4.3: Application wrapped by a service.

(1) First, the user searches for a service repository.

(2) When a repository has been found (externally or from the provider directly), the user searches for a suitable service.

(3) To be able to use the service, the customer needs to find out which software is needed to invoke the service, typically by using a search engine or by searching the website of the provider offering the service.

(4) Then, the user downloads the software and

(5) installs it. The application has to contain a component which acts as a web service client.

(6) Finally, the customer invokes the service.

This solution does not provide a satisfactory integration into a SOA. The user still needs to know where to get the software from, is not able to generate a web service client for the service, and thus still needs the client from the service provider. This introduces an additional software development effort for the service provider.

The third solution is to completely implement the application using web services, as shown in Figure 4.4.

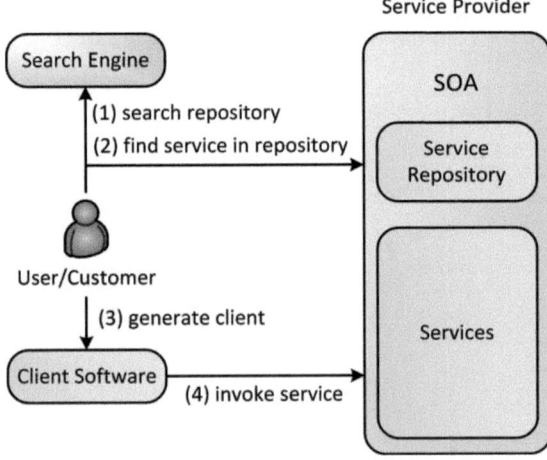

Figure 4.4: Application realized as services.

4.1. Introduction 37

(1) Again, the user searches for a service repository.

(2) When an appropriate repository has been found, the user searches for a suitable service.

(3) From the service description, the client software can be generated automatically,

(4) which then communicates with the service.

In theory, this is the best solution (at least the best of the three), but there are still several problems:

(a) This approach is very costly in terms of time and money, since a complete reimplementation of the legacy application is required.

(b) When the legacy application requires data streaming capabilities, the used protocols' payloads are now transferred over SOAP, which typically generates a large overhead. In a streaming application, web services probably need to manage state (which is already addressed by the Web Services Resource Framework (WSRF) [46]). However, since such an application typically invokes a service repeatedly, a large overhead compared to the message payload is introduced—especially when the messages are short.

(c) Web services cannot be used to integrate legacy applications with real-time requirements into a SOA without inducing a non-negligible processing and communication overhead. It is difficult to still meet guaranteed upper bounds on the processing time after handling a real-time application via SOAP.

(d) Large file transfers can be problematic due to the usually used Base64 encoding, which inflates the original data to a size of 133%. Handling Base64 encodings is quite inflexible and hence better protocols should be used. The Flex-SwA architecture presented in Chapter 5 addresses the performance problem by providing a platform that allows to select suitable protocols, but the protocol selection has to be offered in a standard-based way (e.g., by using WS-Policy [96]).

(e) The requirements of the application need to be described along with the service description to allow an automatic generation of client software.

Therefore, whenever complex legacy applications are used, streaming or real-time requirements occur, or large file transfers are needed, web services are not adequate for describing the requirements of these applications.

The novel communication policy for web services based on WS-Policy combines the advantages of using applications independently of a SOA and implementing/integrating these applications with web services. The communication policy describes the protocols of an application along with the service description, such that a web service client can automatically be generated if it depends on standard protocols or the service user supports the specified protocols. If the application uses a custom protocol, the location of the software to use can be provided and the installation (or at least part of it) can be automated. By providing the opportunity to use the most suitable protocols, the communication policy solves performance and processing problems that would occur if the communication overhead of using SOAP was added.

The problems of integrating applications with streaming, real-time, and file transfer requirements are pointed out in Chapter 9 (see Section 9.4.3) by investigating a video-on-demand application.

4.2 Defining a Communication Policy

To solve the mentioned problems, the idea of using the SOAP protocol for every application in a SOA must be given up. In general, SOAP can be used to invoke a service, but the communication with the service should be handled by using suitable protocols tailored to the application. These protocols should still be based on standards (or quasi-standards). For example, if a file transfer service was used, a SOAP message would be sent to the service and then a protocol like FTP or GridFTP [10] would be used to transfer the file instead of sending the file as part of the SOAP message. For a video conference or a video-on-demand application, the H.323 [3] or the RTP protocol [86] would be used.

Figure 4.5 shows a novel solution for integrating applications with the mentioned characteristics into a SOA based on web services.

(1) A user first searches a repository containing the right type of service and then

(2) searches the repository for the service description containing the proposed communication policy.

(3) With the help of the WSDL and the information of the policy, it is possible to generate client software as long as the protocols described in the communication policy are based on standards. If custom protocols are used, a link to the software can be provided assisting the installation process in a (semi-)automatic way.

(4) The software is used to invoke the service.

To implement this solution, the descriptive power of WSDL has to be extended. Hence, a novel communication policy based on WS-Policy is introduced to expose different protocols that can be used to communicate with a service. The idea of the proposed communication policy is that a service is capable of

4.2. Defining a Communication Policy

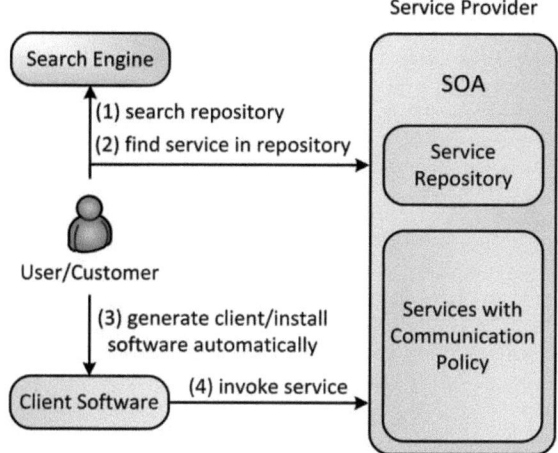

Figure 4.5: Fully integrated application.

describing its means of communication in addition to the WSDL description by providing the necessary information for a web service client to use other protocols to communicate with a service/application (for example real-time protocols) and leverage efficient binary file transfer protocols.

4.2.1 Real-time or Streaming Requirements

If applications require real-time or streaming capabilities, then the communication policy can be used to describe the protocols the client software needs to understand for the interaction with the application. A sample policy file embedding protocol information is shown in Listing 4.1.

```
<wsp:Policy
  xmlns:cp="http://fb12.de/2007/05/communicationpolicy"
  xmlns:wsp="http://www.w3.org/ns/ws-policy">
  <wsp:ExactlyOne>
    <cp:protocol name="RTP" serviceref="VideoOnDemandService"
      protocolID="RTPv2" operationref="streamVideo" />
  </wsp:ExactlyOne>
</wsp:Policy>
```

Listing 4.1: Policy for a real-time service.

The prefix cp describes the namespace of the communication policy. The `protocol` element has up to four attributes: the attribute `name` describes the name of the protocol and is required. The attribute `protocolID` is a unique identifier of the protocol and should be provided, too. This can, for example, be a namespace or a protocol name with a version number. The third attribute can either be `endpointURI` or `serviceref` combined with a fourth attribute `operationref`. The `endpointURI` attribute exposes the endpoint directly with which a communication can take place using the protocol described by the `protocolID`. Every client reading the WSDL description and supporting the given protocol can invoke this endpoint. The `serviceref` attribute refers to a service of which the operation referenced by `operationref` returns an endpoint via which the web service client can communicate with the protocol described by the `protocolID`. By using `serviceref` and `operationref`, an endpoint can be dynamically created on a per client basis. The endpoint is not publicly exposed, but only to the client having invoked the service. If only `operationref` is provided, the operation of the service, the communication policy belongs to, will return the endpoint as if `serviceref` was set to the name of the service itself.

The referenced service could provide an endpoint reference as defined in the WS-Addressing specification [48], thus using a standard way of handling endpoint addresses. Additionally, an integration with, for example, web service security mechanisms is possible, i.e. the communication policy can also be associated with a security policy to handle authentication before allowing access to the newly described applications.

The sample communication policy in Listing 4.1 describes how a service can expose a real-time application. A client invoking the service has to understand the protocol given in the `name` attribute—in the example the RTP protocol. The client initiates the preparation of a real-time communication by sending a SOAP message to the referenced service. After the service has processed the SOAP message, it will start the real-time communication and return the RTP endpoint (`rtp://137.248.121.11:22222/video`, for example). The client's SOAP message could be used to select quality of service parameters, service-level agreements or realizing security aspects.

4.2.2 Legacy Integration

The communication policy works well for applications based on standard protocols. One can reasonably assume that nearly every client can be configured/installed to use a set of standard protocols.

The integration of legacy applications using a complex custom protocol requiring interaction with the client software is more difficult. In this case, often only the provider of the application knows the underlying protocol. The protocol has not been standardized and will in most cases never be. In this situation, the provider must make a client application available to the user. This can be done by adding a link in the communication policy where a client application

4.2. Defining a Communication Policy 41

can be obtained from as shown in Listing 4.2. The client can be an executable directly downloadable by providing a URL, it can be generated by invoking a client generator web service, or it can be a website assisting a human user to invoke a service. This last option is especially useful if the web service is invoked by a human being.

```
<wsp:Policy
  xmlns:cp="http://fb12.de/2007/05/communicationpolicy"
  xmlns:wsp="http://www.w3.org/ns/ws-policy">
  <wsp:ExactlyOne>
    <cp:client name="videoOnDemand" type="download"
      endpointURI="http://downloads.fb12.de/vodClient.zip"/>
  </wsp:ExactlyOne>
</wsp:Policy>
```
Listing 4.2: Link to a sophisticated client.

The **client** tag provides the information to obtain a suitable client application. The **endpointURI** attribute can have different semantics. If the **type** attribute has the value **download**, the endpoint URI is the location where a client application can be downloaded from. If the **type** attribute has the value **generate**, the endpoint URI provides the address of a client generator service. Finally, if the type equals **web**, the URI provides the address of a website via which the service can be invoked with a web browser. The **name** attribute is used to provide the name of the client. Instead of the **endpointURI**, again the **serviceref** and **operationref** attributes can be used to

- specify the service and operation that returns a (perhaps dynamically created) endpoint not being publicly exposed, and to

- allow the integration with other web service specifications.

The communication policy allows a SOA to adopt any type of application as long as it is based on common protocols or a client protocol implementation is provided in the **client** tag. If requirements are needed by the client application, these can be specified by embedding a **requirements** tag into the client tag.

Listing 4.3 shows how to link to a client with specific requirements. At the moment, only operating systems and Java Virtual Machine requirements are provided in the communication policy namespace. The **requirements** tag is embedded into the **client** tag. The **ExactlyOne** element describes that it is enough to fulfill one requirement to make the client application work. **architecture** describes the processor architecture, e.g., x86 or Power PC. **os** describes the operating system and **osversion** the version of the operating system. For example, libraries (in specific versions) needed to execute the client application could also be specified.

```xml
<wsp:Policy
  xmlns:cp="http://fb12.de/ws/2007/05/communicationpolicy"
  xmlns:wsp="http://www.w3.org/ns/ws-policy" >
  <wsp:ExactlyOne>
    <cp:client name="videoOnDemandWinXP" type="download"
      endpointURI="http://downloads.fb12.de/vodClientWinXP.zip">
      <wsp:ExactlyOne>
        <cp:requirements architecture="x86" os="Windows XP"
          osversion="5.1" jvm="1.6.0_06"/>
      </wsp:ExactlyOne>
    </cp:client>
    <cp:client name="videoOnDemandLinux" type="download"
      endpointURI="http://downloads.fb12.de/vodClientLinux.zip">
      <wsp:ExactlyOne>
        <cp:requirements architecture="ppc" os="Linux"
          osversion="2.6.18.2-34-default" />
      </wsp:ExactlyOne>
    </cp:client>
  </wsp:ExactlyOne>
</wsp:Policy>
```

Listing 4.3: Link to a sophisticated client specifying requirements.

Additional requirements can be specified in other namespaces (element-based extensibility), thus allowing the adaption to changing requirements in the future.

4.2.3 Leveraging File Transfers

Furthermore, a communication policy can be used to extend the functionality of a service by offering file transfer capabilities. Large files cannot easily be transferred using SOAP (see, for example, Ying et al. [98]) since they have to be encoded in the body of the SOAP message and processed by the service provider's SOAP engine. By specifying file transfer capabilities, it is possible to leverage effective binary file transfer protocols such as GridFTP. The example in Listing 4.4 shows a communication policy for a data service.

The element `filetransfer` is handled exactly like the `protocol` element except that the `protocol` element indicates that a communication between client and service may take place via the given protocol, whereas the `filetransfer` element indicates the protocols being used to push/pull a file to/from a service. The additional attribute `type` can be set to `pull` if the service "downloads" the data from a client, to `push` if a client "uploads" data to a server, or to `both` if the file transfer is supported in both directions. Again, the file transfer could be coupled with a security policy.

Concretely, the sample communication policy for the data service offers the client to choose one out of five file transfer protocols. For each protocol, the `type` attribute specifies whether the client may push or pull data from the server given

4.2. Defining a Communication Policy 43

```
<wsp:Policy
  xmlns:cp="http://fb12.de/2007/05/communicationpolicy"
  xmlns:wsp="http://www.w3.org/ns/ws-policy">
  <wsp:ExactlyOne>
    <cp:filetransfer name="pastry" type="push"
      endpointURI="P a s t r y I D "/>
    <cp:filetransfer protocolID="http://fb12.de/flexswa"
      name="flexswa" type="both" operationref="getEndpoint"
      serviceref="http://fb12.de:8080/services/DataService"/>
    <cp:filetransfer name="GridFTP" type="both"
      endpointURI="gsiftp://fb12.de:2811"/>
    <cp:filetransfer protocolID="HTTP/1.1" name="http"
      type="pull" endpointURI="http://fb12.de:8092"/>
    <cp:filetransfer name="ftp" type="both"
      endpointURI="ftp://ftp.fb12.de"/>
  </wsp:ExactlyOne>
</wsp:Policy>
```

Listing 4.4: Communication policy for a data service.

by the **endpointURI**. In the example, if the client wants to push data to a server, it may use Pastry, the Flex-SwA file server protocol, GridFTP or FTP. When using the Flex-SwA file server protocol, no endpoint is provided. The operation referenced by **serviceref** and **operationref** has to be invoked. As for real-time and streaming protocols, the service returns an endpoint, which the client may use for file transfers. Otherwise, if the client wants to pull data from the server, it may use HTTP v1.1, FTP, GridFTP, or the Flex-SwA file server protocol.

Providing file transfer capabilities embedded as a policy in WSDL has several advantages:

(a) A suitable protocol can be chosen by the client.

(b) SOAP performance issues are circumvented. If coupled with Flex-SwA, a web or Grid service can directly use the file transferred to the server.

(c) Ordinarily, file transfer is offered by a web or Grid service. For example, if a file transfer service used GridFTP to transfer files, it would have to ensure that the client was able to use GridFTP (as server or client), too. But the need for GridFTP cannot be expressed using standard WSDL. Thus, a file transfer service would have to negotiate this with the client before using a specific protocol. The communication policy, however, clearly states the protocols to be used, such that a client is able to check for compatibility first.

4.3 Summary

A communication policy for web services has been presented for defining nonstandard application requirements for web services. The implementation and integration of legacy applications or applications with particular requirements that cannot be specified by WSDL is now possible. It allows to use the most suitable, efficient protocols for realizing streaming and real-time applications, integrating complex legacy applications (especially if custom protocols are involved), and implementing efficient file transfers, while still integrating such applications into the SOA. A (semi-)automatic generation of client software is possible and the location of suitable clients and their requirements can be described.

Table 4.1 shows an overview of the elements and attributes of the communication policy and their meaning.

The communication policy is used to describe these requirements without (re)implementing an application with web services. Since some applications' requirements can hardly be met when running the application over SOAP, this approach is especially reasonable.

4.3. Summary

Table 4.1: Overview of the communication policy.

Element	Description of element and contained attributes	
	Attributes	Description
protocol	The protocol element describes the protocols the client software needs to understand for the interaction with the application.	
	name	name of the protocol
	protocolID	namespace or version of the protocol
	endpointURI	exposes endpoint for direct communication
	serviceref and operationref	references service and operation returning a dynamically created endpoint for the protocol
filetransfer	The filetransfer element describes the protocols needed to push/pull data to/from a service.	
	name	name of the file transfer protocol
	protocolID	namespace or version of the file transfer protocol
	type	push: client uploads data to server/service pull: service downloads data from a client both: push and pull is possible
	endpointURI	directly exposes endpoint for data transfers
	serviceref and operationref	references service and operation returning a dynamically created endpoint for data transfers
client	The client element provides an endpoint from where to obtain a suitable client.	
	name	name of the client
	ID	namespace identifying the client
	type	download: endpoint refers to the location of the client generate: endpoint refers to a client generator service web: address of website providing client for web browser
	endpointURI	directly exposes endpoint to obtain a client
	serviceref and operationref	references service and operation returning a dynamically created endpoint to obtain a client
requirements	The requirements element is nested into the client element. It describes requirements for the client software.	
	architecture	name of the processor architecture
	os	Name of the operating system
	osversion	Version of the operating system
	jvm	Version of the Java Virtual Machine
	...	Further requirements will be added in the future.

5
Facilitating Flexible Data Transfers

5.1 Introduction

In this chapter, an overview of web service interaction patterns is given and the need for a more flexible and efficient data handling model derived (Figure 5.1). The layer model of the Flex-SwA architecture and different communication patterns are presented providing post-invocation parameter transmission as well as reduced data movement, seamless message forwarding, and overlapping execution of data transmission and service invocation. By using a communication policy to describe data handling capabilities of services, a seamless integration of Flex-SwA is possible; clients consuming services based on the Flex-SwA architecture can identify protocol requirements from the policy. *Parts of this chapter have been published in [55, 73, 87].*

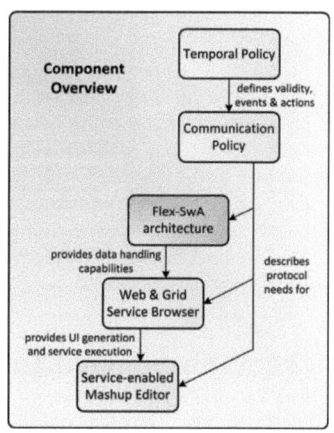

Figure 5.1: Overview: Flex-SwA.

Service-oriented architectures—in particular those based on web services—have been adopted in several fields of applications, e.g., Grid computing [38], enterprise application integration [50], and medical data exploration [44]. These application areas have in common that often large amounts of binary data have to be transferred between different nodes.

To invoke a web or Grid service, SOAP [74] is commonly used. In practice, a service requires several parameters to perform its task, which are embedded in the SOAP message. As long as these parameters are primitive ones such as integers or floating point numbers, or strings, they can be embedded into the SOAP message. A problem occurs if bulk binary data, e.g., bitmap graphics or audio/video files, have to be transmitted or if data has to be repetitively sent to services. SOAP is unsuitable to transmit bulk binary data, since the data have to be encoded before being embedded in the SOAP message to—among others— enable the use of the characters '<' and '>' in the payload of an XML message. When small amounts of data are sent repetitively, the SOAP envelope containing the data induces a huge overhead compared to the size of the payload.

To circumvent the problem of bulk data transfer, the SOAP Messages with Attachments (SwA) specification [20] has been introduced. This specification describes how binary data can be attached to a SOAP message by using Multipurpose Internet Mail Extensions (MIME) messages [41]. A SwA message is actually a MIME multipart/related message containing a SOAP message and one or several attachments, which contain the binary data to be transmitted. Using SwA has a main disadvantage: access to an attachment is only possible if all preceding attachments have been received. Random access to an arbitrary attachment is not possible. Hence, receiving and processing of a multipart message containing various, possibly large, attachments requires a non-negligible amount of time.

To avoid the drawbacks associated with the use of SwA, an architecture for flexibly handling binary data in service-oriented environments called *Flex-SwA* is presented. It is based on references pointing to data locations, which allows message forwarding without additional communication cost and demand-driven evaluation and transmission of binary data. Additionally, Flex-SwA offers (1) several communication patterns, allowing the service developer to focus on service development instead of data transmission and (2) post-invocation parameter transmission (PIPT), empowering a developer to invoke a service and subsequently send parameters to it, i.e. after its invocation.

5.2 Web Service Interaction Patterns

Web service interaction takes place by exchanging SOAP messages. Fundamentally, a SOAP message is a stateless one-way message. By combining one-way message exchanges, more complex interaction patterns can be created, e.g., request/response. These patterns are often based on the client/server-paradigm. Furthermore, SOAP offers two binding styles: `rpc` and `document`. The first one indicates that an operation follows the remote procedure call (RPC) paradigm, i.e. a request message contains parameters, a response message return values. The

5.2. Web Service Interaction Patterns

latter indicates that an operation is document-oriented, i.e. a message contains documents.

Clients perform web service invocation by passing SOAP messages to the server. These messages contain any number of parameters to be passed to the service. Reply messages may be transmitted either synchronously or asynchronously from the server to the client. Figure 5.2 shows an example of a SOAP RPC. The web service client composes a request message containing all necessary parameters and sends it to the web service (1). The web service processes the request, i.e. the desired operation is invoked with the received parameters (2). After the processing of the request message is finished, the web service composes a response message containing the return value. This response message is sent to the web service client (3).

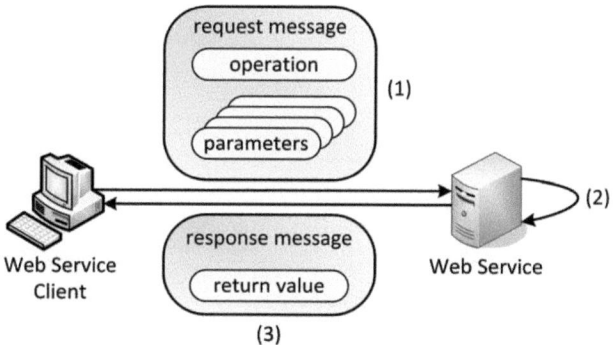

Figure 5.2: An example of a SOAP RPC.

The SOAP protocol defines an XML-based format for the messages to be used in a web service invocation. This XML format cannot handle large binary content well, since it requires an encoding of the content prior to embedding it into a message. For this reason, the SwA specification has been proposed to transmit large binary data objects outside of the XML part. To attach binary objects to a SOAP message, SwA uses MIME multipart/related messages. The SOAP message always resides in the first part of the multipart message. MIME uses a delimiter to separate the different message parts from each other, such that the message must be parsed until the delimiter of the desired part of the message is found. An example MIME message with a web service invocation and two images as attachments is shown in Listing 5.1.

------=_Part_0_21662929.1130315394983-- is the delimiter that is used for this MIME multipart/related message to separate each message part. The first part of the message is the SOAP envelope including the method to invoke.

```
------=_Part_0_21662929.1130315394983
Content-Type: text/xml; charset=UTF-8
Content-Transfer-Encoding: binary
Content-Id: <ED8BBCB74E9A8832E096679A7B3B2829>
<?xml version="1.0" encoding="UTF-8"?>
<env:Envelope
 xmlns:env="http://schemas.xmlsoap.org/soap/envelope/"
 xmlns:xsd="http://www.w3.org/2001/XMLSchema"
 xmlns:xsi="http://www.w3.org/2001/XMLSchema-instance">
 <env:Body>
  <putFile
    env:encodingStyle="http://schemas.xmlsoap.org/soap/encoding/"/>
 </env:Body>
</env:Envelope>
------=_Part_0_21662929.1130315394983
Content-Type: image/gif
Content-Transfer-Encoding: binary
Content-Id: <CE1E2EF092B98740A3FC5EDF67B1308D>
binary data
------=_Part_0_21662929.1130315394983
Content-Type: image/gif
Content-Transfer-Encoding: binary
Content-Id: <1C4EF7B7D9E0EC61045E3D97744CA0F8>
binary data
------=_Part_0_21662929.1130315394983--
```

Listing 5.1: Example of a MIME multipart/related message.

5.3. Flex-SwA Architecture

The second and the third part are images in the Graphics Interchange Format (GIF) sent as attachments; *binary data* represent the data of the images. The message ends with the delimiter.

The general web service interaction pattern using SwA is shown in Figure 5.3. A main disadvantage of this approach is that the server has to wait for the transmission of the entire message before it can decode every attachment part. As a consequence, the transmission of large attachments can take a considerable time, and attachment processing requires large amounts of main or external memory. Depending on the implementation of the underlying web service framework, processing of the SOAP message and invocation of the target service is often deferred until the entire message containing all attachments has been completely received.

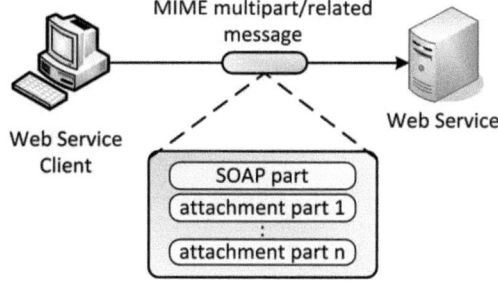

Figure 5.3: General web service interaction pattern using SwA.

In application areas where large amounts of data have to be transferred, these disadvantages are not acceptable. Therefore, other implementation patterns handling the transmission of large amounts of data have been implemented in an application specific manner. A common implementation pattern to be found in such an environment is the transmission of data location pointers (URIs or more complex reference structures), which are interpreted in the application logic of the service. The service implementation then uses other data access technologies, e.g., OGSA-DAI [62] or RFT [91] in Grid environments.

Flex-SwA avoids these disadvantages.

5.3 Flex-SwA Architecture

This section gives an overview of the general architecture of Flex-SwA. The Flex-SwA protocol stack, reference concept, and communication and memory patterns are explained. The section closes with a description of how Flex-SwA reduces data movement and enables seamless message forwarding.

5.3.1 Flex-SwA Protocol Stack

Figure 5.4 shows the entire protocol stack from the service user's and the service provider's point of view.

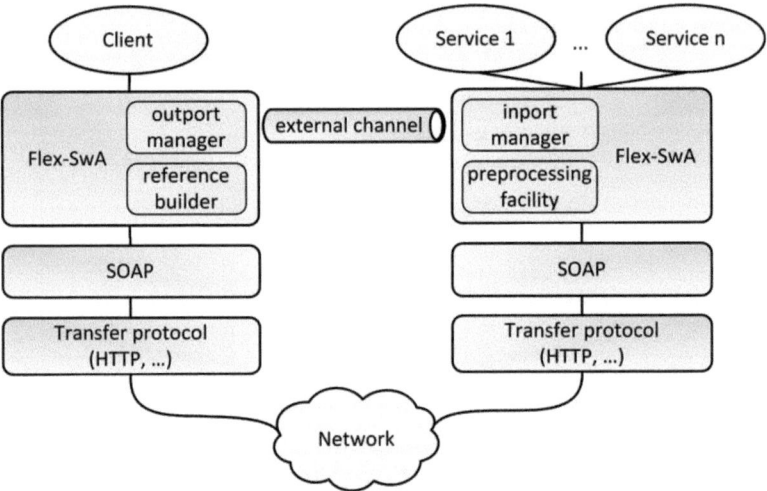

Figure 5.4: The Flex-SwA protocol stack.

Each layer of the protocol stack uses lower layers and offers special functionality to higher layers. The client resides on top of the service user's protocol stack, which is using the Flex-SwA layer to invoke remote services. To transfer bulk binary data, the Flex-SwA layer uses a reference builder to create a reference. A reference is an XML description that refers to the actual location of the bulk data and determines the protocols to use to transfer it. On top of the service provider's protocol stack, several services are offered that are based on the Flex-SwA layer. If service invocations containing references arrive, the preprocessing facility subsequently prepares data transmission for the references received from the client. However, the preprocessing facility does not need to handle every reference. The unhandled references can be forwarded to other service providers, thus providing message forwarding without additional communication cost, since the size of the reference—compared to the data transferred—is very small. Both Flex-SwA layers at the service user's and service provider's site are communicating via ordinary SOAP messages that contain the references, thus enabling the use of Flex-SwA in environments where SwA is not supported, such as in the widely used Globus Toolkit 4.0 [39] for Grid computing. Different transfer protocols can be used, e.g.,

5.3. Flex-SwA Architecture

HTTP. From an application developer's point of view, web service invocation and data transmission remain coupled in a *single* service invocation operation. The concrete behavior of the platform regarding the handling of data transmission and service execution can be controlled by specifying a behavioral policy. As an additional benefit, service developers can use the protocol handling capabilities of Flex-SwA to leverage high performance binary protocols by simply specifying a policy to use them, without having to deal with the protocol details in the application code. Such a policy can be specified as a default behavior for the entire platform (e.g., regarding the selection of a preferred transport protocol) or as a service-specific policy. Binary protocols can be selected for each reference individually. In contrast to a realization in a more traditional application environment where the developer has to handle every aspect of the communication, most of the functionality needed to handle a specific transport mechanism is realized in the Flex-SwA layer.

The inport manager, the outport manager, and the external channel cooperate in a producer/consumer environment to enable post-invocation parameter transmission (PIPT). In such an environment, the client may retrieve an outport from the outport manager to repeatedly send data to a web service already invoked. An invoked web service uses the inport manager to retrieve an inport that is interconnected with the outport of the invoking client via an external channel. An external channel is an abstraction of a transmission channel that can use arbitrary transfer protocols. Typically, an external channel interconnects inports and outports in a 1 : 1 ratio, since a client only invokes one web service. However, it would be possible to relate outports and inports 1 : n, if a client wants to invoke n web services concurrently.

With PIPT it is possible to write web service based applications that allow **stream-based producing/consuming of parameters** and **pipelining**. Stream-based production/consumption of parameters is based on the use of a streaming protocol for data transmission. Consider, for example, a matrix consisting of the columns $\vec{c}_1$ to $\vec{c}_n$. Each column $\vec{c}_1$ to $\vec{c}_n$ can be transferred in its own data package d_1 to d_n one after another. Figure 5.5 shows the situation when the data packages d_1 to d_{n-3} have already been processed by the web service, while d_{n-2} and d_{n-1} are currently transferred and d_n is just being produced by the client application.

Since SOAP messages must be transferred completely before service execution starts, the overall processing time (t_{total}) of a message is the time for producing parameters (t_{prod}), transmitting parameters (t_{trans}), and executing the service (t_{exec}):

$$t_{total} = t_{prod} + t_{trans} + t_{exec}$$

Stream-based production/consumption of parameters allows sending parameters partially (e.g., only one column of a matrix at a time) and processing of already received parameters. Thus, receiving parameters overlaps with service

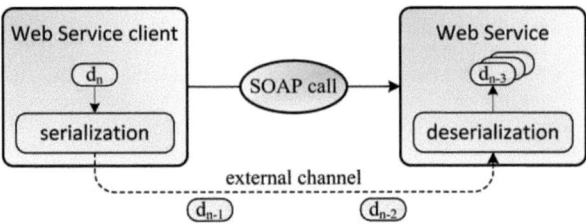

Figure 5.5: Example of stream-based production/consumption of parameters.

execution, and the overall processing time reduces to

$$t'_{total} = t_{prod} + \alpha_t \cdot t_{trans} + \alpha_e \cdot t_{exec} < t_{total}$$

where $\alpha_t, \alpha_e \in (0, 1)$.

As shown in Figure 5.6, the stream-based production/consumption of parameters enables the building of a pipeline between different services/algorithms [90]. Consider n algorithms $a_1, a_2, \ldots, a_n$ with processing times of $t_1, t_2 \ldots, t_n$. Sequential processing leads to an overall processing time of

$$t_{seq} = t_1 + t_2 + \ldots + t_n = \sum_{i=1}^{n} t_i$$

To reduce processing time, a service can send partial results to its successor, which already processes them. The overall processing time is reduced to

$$t_{pipe} = t_1 + \sum_{i=2}^{n} k_i \cdot t_i < t_{seq}$$

where $k_i \in (0, 1), 2 \leq i \leq n$, such that a service a_i saves $(1 - k_i) \cdot t_i$ units of time.

There are two important prerequisites for pipelining: First, each service has to produce partial results that can be processed by its successor. Second, a service has to know where to send the results to. Here, the reference mechanism comes in handy, since a service of the right type can consume the reference, whereas a service of the wrong type may forward the reference to the right kind of service.

Following the service-oriented approach, a WSDL description is used to publish all necessary information about a web service. A simple approach to embed the information in the WSDL description is to use the documentation element. The documentation element contains arbitrary data or XML elements. But using the documentation element violates its intentional semantics to embed human readable information in a WSDL description. Therefore, a better approach is to use a WS-Policy to describe the requirements or capabilities of the web service. In chapter 4, a communication policy is shown capable of describing the protocols a web service depends on.

5.3. Flex-SwA Architecture

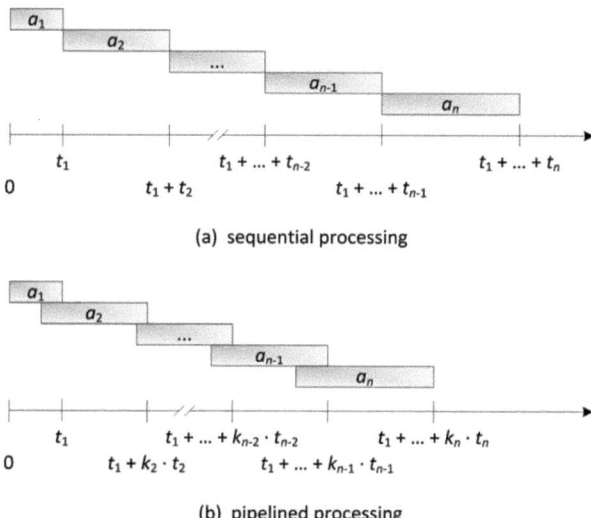

(a) sequential processing

(b) pipelined processing

Figure 5.6: Sequential and pipelined processing.

Both approaches promise compatibility with clients not aware of post-invocation parameter transmission. A client aware of post-invocation parameter transmission parses the service description, encounters the `documentation` element or policy and knows which outports to use to send data via the external channel. All clients not aware of post-invocation parameter transmission simply ignore the element or policy.

The repetitive sending of data is again handled via references, such that a reference can be forwarded to the node(s) that should actually consume the data.

5.3.2 Reference Concept

References in Flex-SwA point to data locations. These data locations can, for instance, be files hosted by third-party servers or the client itself, or buffers in the client's main memory or in the memory of third-party servers. These references are *consumable* or *persistent*. Persistent references can be read again and again, e.g., by different services. The lifetime of these references can, for example, be coupled to the lifetime of the application, of the service instance, of the service itself, or the service engine. Consumable references are references to files that are deleted after they have been successfully read or to memory areas that are deallocated after the reading has been completed. For consumable references, a number of reads can be specified after which they are invalid. References to memory locations can, for example, be represented by a URI containing a UUID.

A reference is transferred in the SOAP message. The definition of the reference in XML Schema is shown in Listing 5.2.

```
<xsd:schema targetNamespace="http://core.flexswa.fb12.de"
  xmlns:xsd="http://www.w3.org/2001/XMLSchema">
  <xsd:complexType name="Reference">
    <xsd:sequence>
      <xsd:element name="resourceURI" type="xsd:string"/>
      <xsd:element name="credential" type="xsd:any"
        minOccurs="0" maxOccurs="unbounded"/>
      <xsd:element name="length" type="xsd:int"
        minOccurs="0" maxOccurs="1"/>
      <xsd:element name="mimeType" type="xsd:string"
        minOccurs="0" maxOccurs="1"/>
      <xsd:element name="suggestedName" type="xsd:string"
        minOccurs="0" maxOccurs="1"/>
      <xsd:element name="consumerType" type="xsd:string"
        minOccurs="0" maxOccurs="1"/>
      <xsd:element name="outportType" type="xsd:string"
        minOccurs="0" maxOccurs="1"/>
      <xsd:element name="extensionElement" type="xsd:any"
        minOccurs="0" maxOccurs="unbounded"/>
    </xsd:sequence>
  </xsd:complexType>
</xsd:schema>
```

Listing 5.2: XML schema for the Flex-SwA reference.

The reference must at least contain a URI describing the access to a resource. All the other elements are optional. Furthermore, it may contain several `credentials` to manage the access to the resource. The `length` attribute can be used to tell the receiving service the size of the referenced data. This information can, for example, be used to decide whether to persist the referenced data or keep it in memory (see section 5.3.4). The `mimeType` can be used to indicate the type of the referenced data. The `suggestedName` is a name for the referenced data, which the service may use if it persists or forwards the data. The `consumerType` indicates a special service type able to consume the reference. `outportType` refers to the outport (if PIPT is used) which writes to the buffer this reference refers to. The `extensionElement` can be used to add arbitrary extensions to the reference.

5.3.3 Communication Patterns

Flex-SwA offers different behaviors related to the transmission of binary data and the execution of services. These are service execution patterns, data transmission

5.3. Flex-SwA Architecture

patterns, concurrency patterns and blocking mode patterns. For each service, a combination of these behaviors can be chosen by the developer of an application.

- **Service Execution Patterns:** There are two possible behaviors regarding the handling of data transmission and execution of a service. In *non-overlapping* mode, the platform performs all data transfers prior to invocation of the service; in *overlapping* mode, data transmission and service execution are performed in parallel. If a service needs to ensure the availability of all data on the service provider's platform before it starts processing, it requests the platform to handle invocations in non-overlapping mode. If initialization of the service requires time and is independent of the data resources referenced, a service developer can specify the service to use overlapping invocation mode, causing the platform to start data transmission and service execution in parallel and thus reducing latency to service execution.

- **Data Transmission Patterns:** The platform can be instructed to perform *eager* or *lazy* transmission of data resources referenced, meaning that references are resolved as soon as possible or only upon a real attempt to access their content. The latter is especially useful when a data resource can be omitted, e.g., if an error has occurred. Additionally, the service can prioritize referenced data resources that are tagged to be transmitted in eager mode, leading to a transmission plan for these.

- **Concurrency Patterns:** Data resources can be transmitted in an *iterative* or *concurrent* fashion. If data resources are transmitted iteratively, only one data resource at a time is retrieved. If the data resources are transmitted concurrently, all data resources are retrieved in parallel.

- **Blocking Mode Patterns:** Two blocking mode patterns are offered: *blocking* and *non-blocking*. If a service is in blocking mode, it requests the retrieval of a data resource and waits until it is fully available. If a service is in non-blocking mode, service execution resumes directly after the retrieval request.

The reasonable combinations of the data transmission, service execution, concurrency and blocking mode patterns are shown in Figure 5.7.

A combination of non-overlapping transmission handling and the eager transmission mode (Figure 5.7(a)) results in transferring every data resource before the service starts. This scheme is similar to the original transmission via SwA. Transmission of the data resources can also be done concurrently (Figure 5.7(b)), for example, by using several threads, thus providing the possibility of improving the transfer rate. Combining overlapping and eager transmission handling (Figure 5.7(c)) results in the immediate start of data transmission and the service. This mode is useful if the service has a certain warm-up time or does not

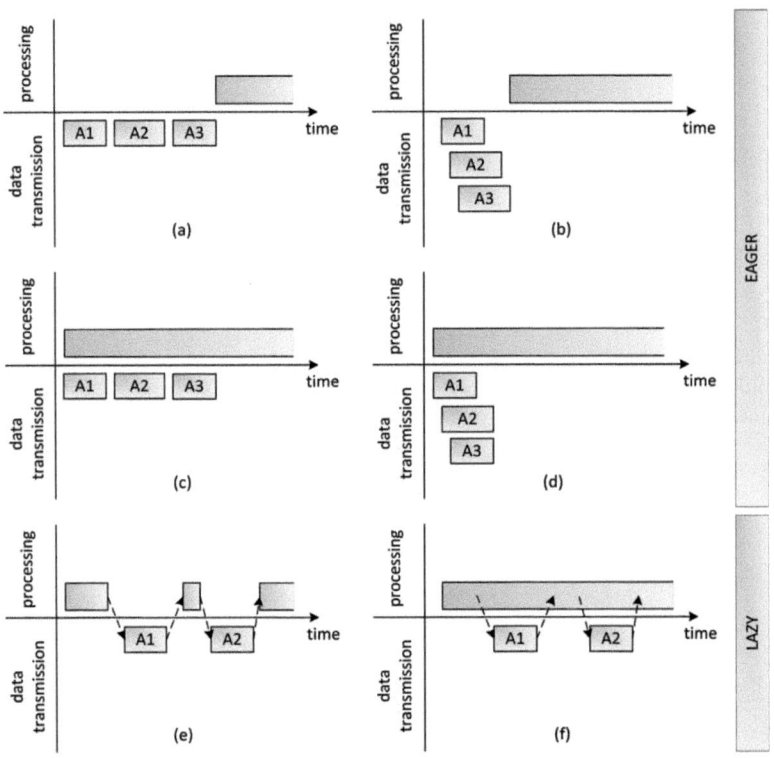

Figure 5.7: Communication patterns in Flex-SwA.

5.3. Flex-SwA Architecture

need any data resources at service start. Here again, a concurrent transmission of data resources (Figure 5.7(d)) possibly provides a better transfer rate than the iterative approach. Lazy data transmission in combination with overlapping transmission handling results in an on-demand transmission of data resources. If the service needs a data resource, transmission is triggered at that time. This can be done in a blocking manner (Figure 5.7(e)), i.e. the service is blocked until data is retrieved from the remote source and stored locally by the infrastructure or in a non-blocking manner (Figure 5.7(f)), i.e. the service only triggers the transmission and continues directly; transferred data may be accessed by the service upon reception. Blocking mode is used if the service needs the complete data resource before the service can resume execution. Non-blocking mode can be used if only a part of the data resource is needed by the service, e.g., an IDEA algorithm [65] needs the next 8-byte blocks for encryption. These service execution patterns enable the demand-driven evaluation and transmission of binary data.

5.3.4 Memory Patterns

In addition to the communication patterns, a service can be configured to persist data as a file prior to accessing the data or to keep the data in memory. Direct memory access promises a faster processing of the data while persisting data has the advantage that huge amounts of data can be handled better since disk space is available in larger amounts than main memory.

5.3.5 Compatibility

A crucial requirement for Flex-SwA is interoperability with existing web service engines using SOAP or SwA. A design aspect of the Flex-SwA architecture is that it must not interfere with the SOAP or SwA handling of a web service engine.

Web service clients need a way to find out whether a service supports Flex-SwA and or not. If the engine does not support Flex-SwA, the client has to transmit data in the SOAP message or as a standard attachment without resorting to other transport protocols. If Flex-SwA is supported the service description is used to inform the client about the service capabilities. While the service description can be interpreted by Flex-SwA aware clients, standard web service clients will ignore the `documentation` elements or communication policy.

In addition to the information that a service supports Flex-SwA, the client also needs to know the concrete protocols the service supports. In general, this property is platform dependent and might vary over time, i.e. some protocols might only be accessible at a certain time. To describe requirements and capabilities that vary over time, WS-TemporalPolicy has been introduced in Chapter 3. If the service interface description is generated on request prior to a service call, these protocol capabilities may also be embedded in the WSDL document. The interface definition may, however, be prefetched and cached in the client, depending on the application needs. Therefore, the Flex-SwA platform can be configured to embed protocol information in dynamically generated WSDL descriptions as well as provide them through a special web service that Flex-SwA clients can query to determine a suitable protocol on demand.

5.3.6 Protocol Decision

Some transport protocols may require preparation overhead. For example, consider the transmission of binary data objects via a GridFTP [9] server that is shared by both service provider and service user. In this scenario, the client has to upload the data to the GridFTP server before the service provider can access the data and retrieve it from the GridFTP server. Other protocols that enable access to the data resource from the client node do not require such a preparation overhead. Service developers can specify a priority order for acceptable protocols for data transmission. The client calculates the intersection of the sets of protocols that both client and service support. It may then decide to make the data resource available by any number of protocols in the order of protocol preference expressed by the service. At least one protocol must be supported.

5.3.7 Reduced Data Movement

If a client invokes a web service, it may send a reference pointing to a location where the service may retrieve its input data from. If the client does not host the data itself, half of the communication cost is saved, as shown in Figure 5.8. In Figure 5.8(a), the client retrieves the data (1) and then sends the data as part of the service invocation (2). Thus, the same data is sent twice. In Figure 5.8(b), only a reference pointing to the location of the data resource is sent to the service (1). The service then retrieves the data resource (2). The data needs only be transferred once. Thus, nearly half of the communication costs are saved.

5.3.8 Seamless Message Forwarding

Flex-SwA offers the opportunity to forward messages to another node without having to transfer the referenced file twice. This mechanism can, for example, be used in reaction to overload situations. The message containing the reference is simply forwarded instead of the data resource. The service actually processing the file will retrieve it. A preprocessing facility may make this decision if an eager pattern is used or even the service itself when a lazy pattern is used.

Figure 5.8(c) shows a client sending multiple references to a service provider (1). The first service provider decides to let a second service provider handle part of the references (2) and processes the remaining parts itself (3). It is not required to process the data for the forwarded references. The second service provider

5.3. Flex-SwA Architecture

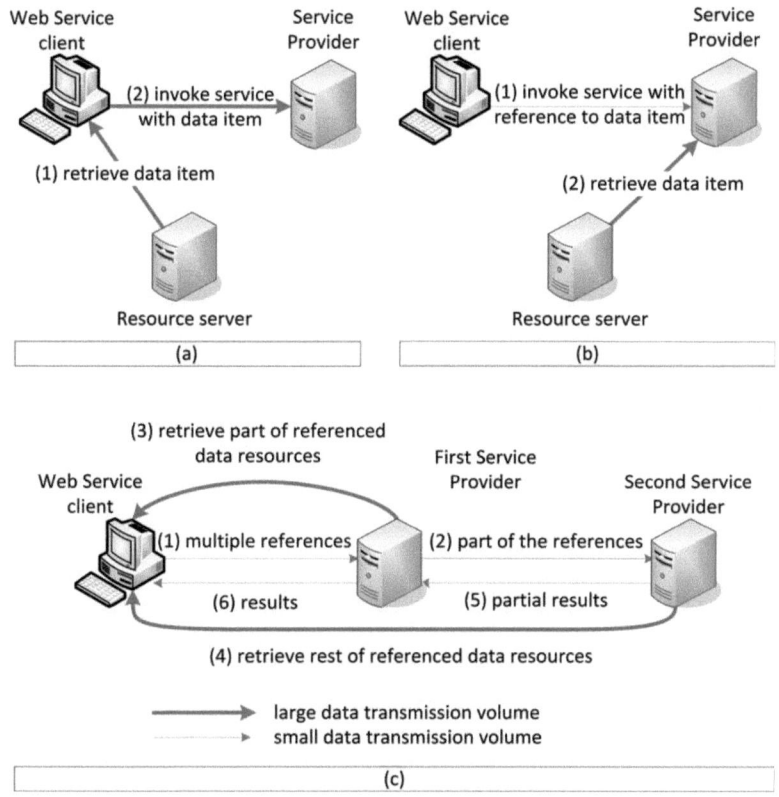

Figure 5.8: Reduced data movement and seamless message forwarding.

resolves its references (4) and provides the results for the handled references (5). The first service provider then returns the collected results (6).

5.4 Summary

Flex-SwA enables a flexible exchange of binary data. Compared to SOAP, no expensive encoding and decoding is necessary, which results in less data to transfer since efficient protocols can be selected. The reference concept permits reduced data movement and the seamless forwarding of messages, useful for load balancing, for example. An overlapping execution of data transmission and service invocation is possible by configuring a service to use the communication patterns. Memory patterns offer to persist files or to keep them in memory for a more efficient processing. Furthermore, the repetitive sending of data to a service is possible (post-invocation parameter transmission). Again, efficient protocols can be used for the transmission of the post-invocation data.

6
Enabling Simple Service Use

6.1 Introduction

In this chapter, a Web and Grid Service Browser is introduced (Figure 6.1) as a familiar entry point for users to easily invoke web and Grid services. An overview of the different web services styles that should reasonably be supported by the browser is shown and the design of the browser components is presented. The use of the communication policy allows to describe the binary protocols a service offers for data transfers, thus enabling the Web and Grid Service Browser to determine whether the service supports a suitable protocol for file uploads. *Parts of this chapter have been published in [54, 51].*

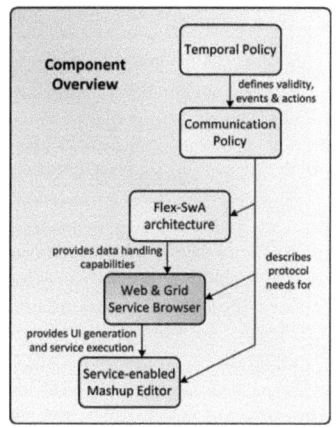

Figure 6.1: Overview: Web and Grid Service Browser.

Service-oriented Grid Computing is not only very popular in the scientific community, but it more and more attracts industrial and even private users. Applications are developed in a standardized manner, consisting of several services based on standards like SOAP, WSDL and in the Grid context the Web Services Resource Framework (WSRF) [46]. But one major problem of Grid services as well as web services is the interface to the users working with the services.

Client programs have to be written, often including a graphical user interface.

63

If a service provider does not offer a client for its services, it is impossible for a user without programming experience to use it. Even portals do not solve this problem, since they only provide an interface to web and Grid service clients and not directly to the services, such that the clients still have to be developed.

Furthermore, the transfer of large data sets is a problem. If done via SOAP, data transmission and service invocation are performed in a single step, but the processing of SOAP messages is very memory- and time-consuming. Consequently, service invocation and data transmission has been divided into two steps. In the first step, data and sometimes executables are moved to the service location. In the second step, the service is invoked and then works with the data (e.g., by executing the binaries). Since the service invocation can only be started after the data has arrived at the service location, moving large amounts of data results in the user waiting a non-negligible amount of time, before (s)he can eventually invoke the service. Furthermore, the user has to *learn* how to transfer the data to the service location. The difficulty of this task ranges from quite simple to fairly complex depending on the transfer method used. Probably, the simplest way of sending data is opening a SSH session to the target node and then transferring the data via SFTP, which is easy for computer scientists, but may be hard for computer novices. A wide-spread but more complex alternative in the Grid area is GridFTP. Using GridFTP, the user has to learn how to generate a proxy certificate and how to use the command line GridFTP client to transfer data. The use of GridFTP is alleviated by using a portal like Gridsphere [92].

Either way, the user has to know where the data has to be sent to and how to achieve this. Both problems, the lack of a (public) client to call existing services and the problem of how and where to transfer data, complicate the use of web and Grid services for new users considerably.

To solve these problems, a Web and Grid Service Browser as a familiar environment for accessing service-oriented environments is introduced. When a user browses to a WSDL description of a service, a graphical frontend is generated, via which the user is able to easily invoke the service. From the view of the user, data transfers are handled as usual. In the background, an implementation of the Flex-SwA architecture (see Chapter 5) has been integrated into the Web and Grid Service Browser and is used to efficiently transmit the data in the same step as the service invocation takes place. Thus, the user is able to "enter" and use the Grid with significantly less effort. Web services can easily be invoked. Since web and Grid service clients are automatically generated on the fly, there is no need for the service developer to develop a graphical user interface for the service user anymore. The service provider does not need to host and maintain a portal.

6.2 Supported Web Service Styles

To build a robust Web and Grid Service Browser, the different combinations of the *binding* styles and *use* attributes should be taken into account [25]:

- RPC/encoded
- RPC/literal
- document/encoded
- document/literal
- document/literal wrapped

All of these styles have advantages and disadvantages. The style/use combination *document/encoded* does not need to be integrated because it is not used in practice [25] and not WS-I compliant[1].

The combination *RPC/encoded* provides the name of the operation to invoke and the message parts (parameters in a programming language) with encoding information and is therefore a very easy-to-use style because the WSDL description is simple and the dispatching to a function/method can easily be done by name. This style is, for example, used by the web service engine Apache Axis, although it is not WS-I compliant. The encoding information is normally unnecessary, when parameter types are already described in the WSDL (which usually is the case), and inflates the SOAP messages. An advantage of the encoded style is that references can be used, which allows to reference the same element twice (or more times) in the same SOAP message. Neither of the other styles uses references.

The *RPC/literal* style is similar to the *RPC/encoded* style but leaves out the encoding information in the SOAP message and is WS-I compliant.

The *document/literal* style provides the message parts for the operation but does not explicitly state the method/function to which a SOAP message should be dispatched. This means that the dispatching is based on the contents of the SOAP body which may only contain one element to be WS-I compliant. To enable an easy dispatching mechanism, the type of the element in the SOAP body should be different for each operation offered by a web service. If more than one parameter is used, these parameters have to be wrapped in a single element. The advantage of this style is (like *RPC/literal*) that type encodings are not transferred in the SOAP message resulting in smaller SOAP messages and a validation of the SOAP message is possible since the WSDL element names are directly used for the parameters.

---

[1]Web Services Interoperability (WS-I) [1] describes a Basic Profile [18] consisting of a set of Web Service specification versions and some additional definitions to make web service implementations, fulfilling this Basic Profile, interoperable.

The most often used style/use combination is *document/literal wrapped* (particularly in the Grid community). This style is also the most flexible one. The operation name is provided like in the RPC styles while the WSDL elements are used as parameters. The main disadvantage of this style/use combination is that overloaded methods cannot be displayed in an automatically generated WSDL. The web service engine needs a dispatching mechanism that allows to map WSDL operations to functions/methods (if the names of the operation and functions/methods differ), which is not too complicated. Another disadvantage is that the WSDL is much more complicated. But since WSDL descriptions should be generated automatically and not read by humans, this is no problem, when tools for this tasks have been successfully built.

Hence, the most important style to support is *document/literal wrapped*. But the other styles except *document/encoded* may also be quite important to support a wide coverage of web services.

6.3 The Web and Grid Service Browser

To invoke a web service, normally a user has to install a web service engine and write client software, for example, by generating stubs from the WSDL description and using these to program the client software. To use the client software, a compiler and or interpreter of the used programming language is needed.

In case of a Grid service, the user normally has to download Grid middleware like the Globus Toolkit, Unicore, or gLite, unzip and/or install it, probably set a few environment variables, read the middleware documentation to program a client able to invoke the service, compile the client with the correct dependencies, and start the client. If Grid middleware like the Globus Toolkit 4.x is involved, the user has to have deep knowledge of the security mechanisms of the middleware.

The goal of the *Web and Grid Service Browser* is to alleviate the user from all the steps mentioned and make access to web and Grid services as easy as browsing the web. Therefore, several requirements have to be satisfied to build the browser.

- First, users need to be able to find services. In the Grid context, this is mainly done by browsing repositories. Thus, a Grid service search engine that is connected to several repositories is needed, so that the repositories do not need to be searched one by one. In the web service context, there are already search engines for web services like Woogle [33] and the Web Service Crawler Engine [8], which could be integrated. Thus, the focus is laid on the development of a Grid service search engine.

- Second, the user needs to be able to provide the parameters for the service to be invoked. Therefore, a graphical user interface has to be created from the WSDL description. The browser needs to be capable of visualizing the

6.3. The Web and Grid Service Browser

elements described, thus making it possible for human users to select their service and operation, fill out a generated form, set security settings if not described by the service and invoke the service.

- Third, the parameters have to be serialized and put into a SOAP message. Since web and Grid services are based on open standards such as SOAP and WSDL (and Grid services on other WS-specifications such as WS-Security [77], WS-SecureConversation [14], WS-Addressing [48], Web Services Resource Framework [46], etc.), the browser needs access to (or a (partial) reimplementation of) an extensive web and Grid service stack implementing these specifications.

- Fourth, a way of handling large amounts of data has to be integrated into the Web and Grid Services Browser. The data transfer and service invocation should be done in a single step. For this task, the Flex-SwA architecture provides a well suited framework for dealing with large amounts of data in service-oriented environments.

- Fifth, the result has to be displayed in a user-friendly, human-readable manner.

Figure 6.2 shows a typical sequence of actions, from searching and selecting the service, to displaying the results.

The user sends a query to a web or Grid service search engine (1), and several matching results are returned (2). After selecting the service to invoke, the WSDL document is requested by the browser (3) and returned to the browser extension (4). The extension lets a User Interface Generator Service interpret the WSDL description (5) and provide a graphical description of the input parameters needed by the service (6). The graphical description is displayed in the browser and the user is required to enter the information needed to invoke the service (7). The data for service invocation is submitted to an Execution Engine (8), which then invokes the web or Grid service (9). The result (10) is returned to the execution engine and handed back to the browser extension (11) which invokes a Result Presentation Service (12). The generated graphical representation of the result is returned to the browser extension (13). The browser extension hands the values back to the browser (14). Finally, the user may rate the service (15) to help other users in the selection of services.

Some of the steps and components are examined more closely in the following sections.

6.3.1 Grid Services Search Engine

A Grid user leverages the Grid service search engine to see whether services (s)he is interested in already exist. The search engine should be conceptually located

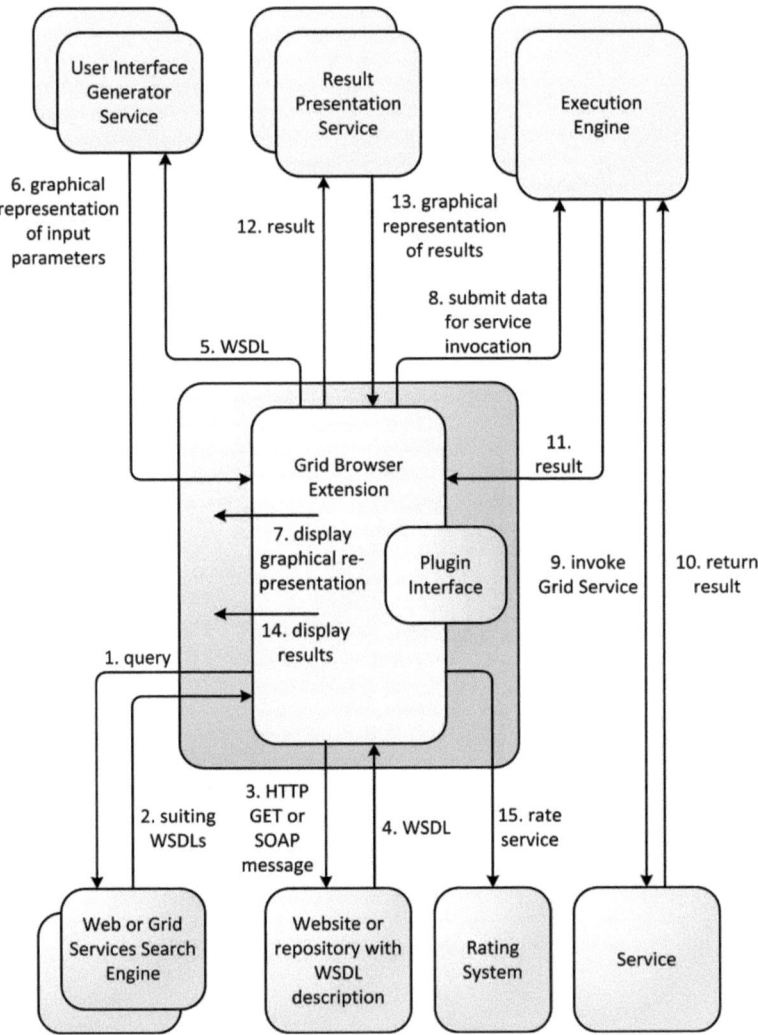

Figure 6.2: Invoking a service from the Web and Grid Service Browser.

6.3. The Web and Grid Service Browser

on remote servers to allow full concentration on (1) "crawling" Grid repositories and Grid nodes for services and (2) caching those services to provide a faster search. A search engine can use different strategies to find services. The first one is to use existing search engines like Google. But with web search engines, it is hard to find descriptions of Grid services. The second strategy is to search existing Grid service repositories. This works well as far as services are registered in repositories and the repositories are known to the search engine. The third possibility is to query the Grid nodes directly whether they offer services.

The Grid services found by the search engine at least include the location of the service endpoint and the name of the service. If the WSDL description contains documentation tags with human-readable information, this information should additionally be provided by the search engine to allow an easier selection of the service.

To provide further information on whose account human beings can make decisions, *tags*, *descriptions*, and *ratings* with *reviews* of services can be provided. *Tags* comprise simple words via which services can be described, for example, a service for detecting faces in videos might use the following words as tags: `face detection`, `OpenCV`, `Viola`, `Jones`, `video`, `MPEG`. `Face detection` describes the purpose of the service, `OpenCV`, `Viola`, and `Jones` describe that the face detection algorithm is taken from the OpenCV [59] library and the algorithm of Viola and Jones [97] is used. `Video` and `MPEG` describe that this algorithm operates on videos, more precisely, on MPEG videos. A `description`, however, gives a more precise description on what the service does—written in prose. *Ratings* and *reviews* can be shown to potential users of the service. They may help to provide information on how to use the service and indicate whether the service could satisfy its users.

6.3.2 User Interface Generator Service

To avoid that every service provider has to offer a web interface on their servers and/or a client able to invoke their services, a facility that generates a graphical user interface from the WSDL description of a service is needed. For this reason, a User Interface (UI) Generator Service is used being either a service on the web or directly integrated into the browser. This allows a user to choose between local (client-side) processing and remote (server-side) processing and also to select different providers with respect to which graphical representation (s)he likes best for service invocation.

From the `types` section of the WSDL description, different fields can be created. By using the XML Schema `appInfo` element or the `documentation` tag of XML Schema or WSDL, information can be provided about which graphical element to use for which field and which texts to display to help the user fill out the forms. If a *Reference* type from Flex-SwA is used, the Web and Grid Service Browser uses Flex-SwA's data transfer capabilities.

6.3.3 Execution Engine

After providing the parameters needed by the service, the service has to be invoked. This can be done by an Execution Engine, which again can be a local or remote component. Local processing may have the advantage that data does not have to be transferred to the Execution Engine and then again to the service. To transfer data from the browser to the Execution Engine, SOAP is a good choice, because then there is no need to encode the data at the Execution Engine again.

Adding SOAP capabilities to the browser can be done by implementing a SOAP stack for the browser, by using a SOAP stack in one of the languages the browser understands and reimplementing missing Grid functionality, or by executing existing code of an existing SOAP stack written in another language from the browser.

6.3.4 Result Presentation and Visualization

When the result is returned, it has to be displayed in a human-readable manner. This is done by the Result Presentation Service. It generates graphical elements from the WSDL description looking at the operations' output messages. This service can again be executed locally or remotely allowing the user to select a provider with the best suiting graphical representations. Here again, annotations, an `appinfo` tag, or a `documentation` tag can be provided to help the presentation service choose the best graphical element to represent the content of the message. For complex computation results, it may be necessary to implement applications for the visualization of the result. To plug the visualization application into the browser, a plugin interface is provided.

6.3.5 Rating System

A browser in the Web 2.0 age must be able to offer means of communication for its user communities. Service users have the opportunity to rate the services they have used and leave comments to services for future users.

The rating system should be a centralized component maintaining all the ratings. The rating can be used to distinguish between responsible providers with clear service descriptions and providers who violate their promised service quality. The comments may even help to use services, if the documentation of a service is poor or not available.

6.4 Summary

In this chapter, the Web and Grid Service Browser has been introduced as a familiar entry point for end users to "enter" and use a service-oriented Grid and to easily invoke web services. The Web and Grid Service Browser extends the

6.4. Summary

functionality of portals and renders WSDL files directly in addition to normal HTML files, so that a service developer does not need to develop a client anymore and a service provider does not need to host and maintain a portal. For the end user, a graphical frontend that eases the invocation of web and Grid services or the submission of a job is generated. A user does not need to create a client programmatically anymore. Data transfers are integrated into the service invocation using an implementation of the Flex-SwA architecture, so that a user does not need to know the location (s)he has to transfer data to and does not need to learn how to use data transfer mechanisms like SSH or GridFTP.

7
Leveraging Grid Resources for End User Development

7.1 Introduction

In this chapter, a Service-enabled Mashup Editor (Figure 7.1) that combines the use of popular web applications with high performance computing resources focusing on simplicity and ease of use is introduced. To leverage Grid and Cloud resources, the mashup editor is able to invoke web and Grid services. Data transfers can be described by using a communication policy and implemented by using Flex-SwA. With the temporal policy in combination with a policy for pricing services, it may be possible in the future to dynamically price resources dependent on the infrastructure they are executed on. *Parts of this chapter have been published in [52].*

High performance computing resources can even be attractive to end users and not only to domain experts and computer scientists. One of the greatest obstacles for the end user is that high performance resources

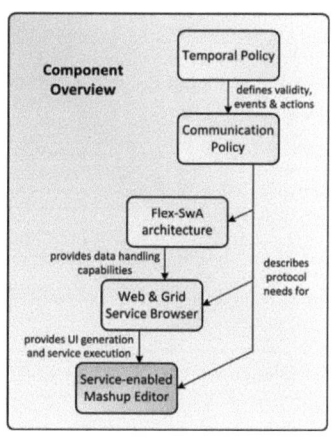

Figure 7.1: Overview: Service-enabled Mashup Editor.

in the form of Grid services or Cloud web services (see, for example, Amazon Elastic Compute Cloud (Amazon EC2) [12]) have the disadvantages (clients have to be written, etc.) as described in Chapter 6. To use such services or even combine services, a mashup editor is a good way for end users to develop their own applications, since the main focus of mashups is simplicity, ease of use, and simple access. Resource-intensive services can be combined to new applications. With the communication policy and the Flex-SwA framework, it is possible to interconnect web and Grid services with popular web applications. The services describe their means of communication with a communication policy. The mashup editor is able to use Flex-SwA references to allow an efficient data transfer to and from services.

7.2 Mashup Editor Classification

Several mashup editors are already available (e.g., Yahoo Pipes (http://pipes.yahoo.com/pipes), Intel Mash Maker (http://mashmaker.intel.com/web/), Microsoft Popfly (http://www.popfly.com/mashupcreator), to name a few). Comparing the features offered by these editors allows to make a classification [99] according to the environment, the component model, and the composition model.

7.2.1 Environment

The *environment* specifies the support a mashup editor provides for the developer and the user. The support of the *development environment* depends on the *interface/modeling paradigm* (visual drag&drop, textual editor, combination of both) and the target group (end users, technically experienced/advanced users, programmers). The *runtime environment* supports the user in the deployment task (standalone, or as a web application) and dictates the processing (client-side, server-side).

7.2.2 Component Model

The *component model* describes the nature of the components, particularly the type, interfaces, and extensibility of the components. Three different *types* for a component can be distinguished:

- data (the component is a pure data source (RSS feed, XML file, etc.)
- application logic (the component is a web service, a web application, etc.)
- user interface (the component interacts with the user)

Also, the component's *interface* can be defined in several ways, for example, with WSDL, IDL, REST, or it can be represented with a GUI. Regarding *extensibility*, components may be

- pre-defined and fixed (allowing no modifications),
- flexible (components can be reconfigured),
- extensible (new operations can be added to existing components).

7.2.3 Composition Model

The *composition model* describes how components can be arranged to form an actual mashup application. The composition can be described by its output type, orchestration style, and data-passing style. The *output type* is, again, data, application logic, or user interface. For the *orchestration* style, three different styles are possible:

- flow-based (tasks are ordered sequentially, e.g., like in a flow chart)
- event-based (e.g., via a publish/subscribe model allowing simple synchronization between tasks)
- layout-based (layout determines order of tasks)

Furthermore, the *data-passing* style describes the flow of the data between the components. Either, the data flows from component to component or the data is written to variables that are then used as the input for other components.

7.3 Service-enabled Mashup Editor

The goal of the *Service-enabled Mashup Editor* is to provide an easy-to-use front end for a set of services consisting of web applications such as YouTube, Flickr, GoogleMaps, etc., web services, and Grid services. In contrast to other mashup editors, the Service-enabled Mashup Editor allows the use of web and Grid services with popular web applications. Users may leverage Grid and Cloud resources in their applications.

Components are generally *flexible UI components* with a data interface for input, a local or remote application logic component and a data interface for output. In contrast to, for example, Yahoo Pipes, where component output is pure data, managed by an RSS feed, components with a UI are more easily readable for human users, thus providing better usability. The compositions are *event-based*. Each time a result of a single component arrives, an event is triggered allowing the next component to exploit the result.

Figure 7.2 shows the environment and the backend of the Service-enabled Mashup Editor.

The *Mashup Editor* is hosted by a *web container* as a Rich Internet Application, so that users do not have to perform complex installations. The client

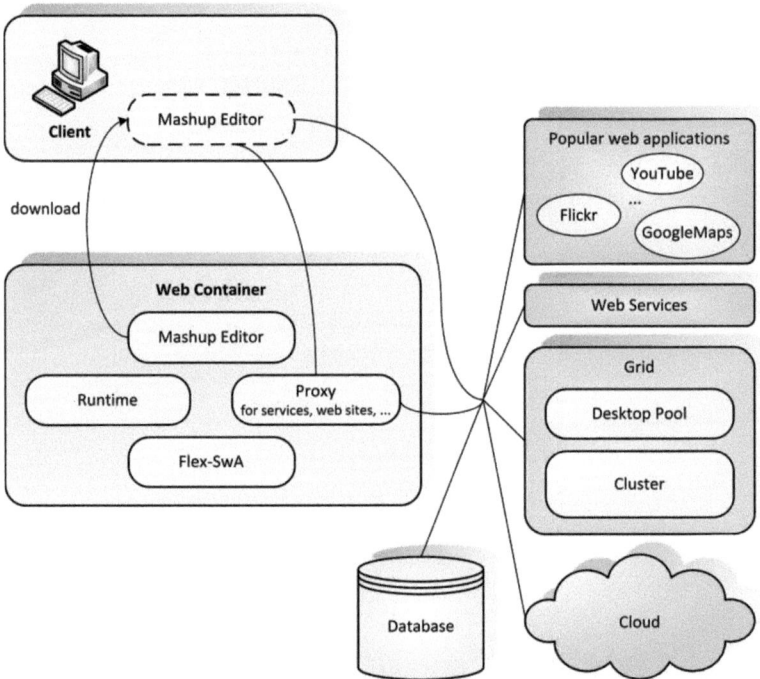

Figure 7.2: Overview of the Service-enabled Mashup Editor.

7.3. Service-enabled Mashup Editor 77

downloads the mashup editor and interacts with services, web applications, etc. The web container also provides a *proxy* that performs tasks from server-side like service invocation, database interaction, etc. whenever this is more reasonable, e.g., for authentication purposes. This is particularly useful in Grid environments where users are burdened to manage their Grid certificates and proxy certificates. For data transfers, *Flex-SwA* can be used when supported by the services.

The use of web and Grid services enables the connection to Grid and Cloud resources. Leveraging these resources is especially useful in contexts with long running tasks, for example, in the area of multimedia applications where shot boundary detection, cut detection, and face detection algorithms already need several minutes even for small videos that are only a few minutes long. The support of web services allows the use of Cloud resources like Amazon EC2 [12]. The support of Grid services allows the use of a cluster (or desktop resources running a Grid middleware). From a user's perspective, the use of Grid and Cloud resources is hidden. (S)he does not have to deal with problems related to the use of these resources.

Furthermore, it is not only possible to create mashups from existing Web 2.0 applications but also to analyze the data used in these applications due to the connection to high performance computing resources. For example, after searching videos, the analysis of shots or actors in this video is also possible.

7.3.1 Scalability

Server-side scalability of the editor is achieved due to the use of Grid and Cloud resources. When more compute resources are needed, the acquisition of such resources is possible.

Client-side scalability can be achieved by using client-side browser technologies like Adobe Flex, Adobe Flash, Microsoft Silverlight, JavaScript, etc. for the implementation of the mashup editor, such that it is downloaded and executed on the client machine.

7.3.2 Views

In contrast to editors like Yahoo Pipes (which only provides a clear developer view) and Intel Mash Maker (which rather provides a user view), the Service-enabled Mashup Editor provides two views, one for the developer and one for the user.

In the *developer view*, new compositions can be defined, saved as new components, and then used for later applications. The components are saved as UI components. The UI is built from the user input of the first component and the output of the last component of the composition. Newly built components can be saved in three different ways:

1. The composition is saved by saving the execution order of the single components in the composition.

2. A new component is generated from the components in the composition, compiled, and dynamically loaded.

3. A BPEL workflow is generated and exposed as a web service. The web service can be used in a headless fashion (even independent of the mashup editor), via a generic web service component, or via a generated UI component.

When the components are saved, they can be assigned to a domain-specific view. For example, there could be components for the multimedia domain and these components could further be divided into categories like video, text, and audio.

The UI for the composition is generated from the input and the output of the components. Each input of a component that is not matched with an output is part of the generated input UI. Each output that is not used as an input for the next component is part of the output UI. Input UI and output UI are combined to build the overall UI of the newly built component.

An application developer mostly handles specific parts of the output of one component and supplies other components with it. (S)he deals mainly with result sets, i.e. with arrays or lists of one type of data like images, videos, etc.

In the *user view*, the user may define his/her applications from existing components. These can be basic components from the editor or components developed in the developer view. The user is also able to switch between different domain-specific views. Instead of working on the large scale (with arrays of images and videos), the user works with concrete search results like single videos, images, audio files etc.

7.3.3 Export to BPEL

The export of components as BPEL services offers one step towards a convergence of workflows and mashups. The service can be used from a BPEL workflow editor as well as from the mashup editor. A possible format for the saved components could be the BPEL4WS language enhanced by descriptions for the visualization.

7.4 Summary

In this chapter, a Service-enabled Mashup Editor that allows the use of Grid or Cloud resources via web and Grid services has been introduced. Thus, it is possible to combine popular web applications like Flickr, YouTube, etc. with services that need high performance computing resources. Not only is the creation of Web 2.0 applications possible, but also the *analysis* of Web 2.0 data. The

7.4. Summary

separation of the view into a user and developer view allows both—the user and the developer—to easily work with the editor.

8
Implementation

8.1 Introduction

This chapter describes the implementation of the different components introduced in this thesis.

Most of the implementation was done in Java 5, Java 6, JavaScript, and Adobe Flex. As a web service engine, Apache Axis 1.4 was used (with Apache Tomcat 5.5.9 or newer as a web server and servlet engine). As a Grid service engine, the Globus Toolkit 4.0.x was used. The Flex-SwA implementation was also tested on Jetty 5.

Since most implemented components use the Apache Axis framework in one way or another and the Globus Toolkit is built on top of the Axis framework, a short introduction to the framework is given in Section 8.2. Moreover, because WS-Policies are based on XML, a transformation from XML to a Java model is reasonable. For these transformations, a XML2Java model generator has been built and is introduced after the introduction to Axis in Section 8.3. After these basic tools, the implementation of the components introduced in this thesis are provided. *Parts of this chapter have been published in [72, 55, 73, 87, 53, 54].*

8.2 Introduction to the Apache Axis Framework

Axis' main purpose is to handle the transfer and processing of SOAP messages. It provides a server and a client both consisting of a set of handler chains. Each handler is capable of changing an incoming or outgoing message and passing it to the next handler in the chain. This enables pre- and postprocessing of incoming or outgoing messages. Handlers pass messages in a so-called message context that holds additional information. A chain is a composition of handlers and other chains. Three chains are predefined in the Axis client and server: the transport chain, the global chain and a chain where the service resides. The server-side engine is structured as shown in Figure 8.1(a).

When a message arrives at the server, it is passed through the transport, global, and service chain. First, it is put into a message context that is forwarded to the transport chain. The transport chain handles transport specific issues, like the protocol used to send the SOAP message (HTTP by default). Then, the message context is forwarded to the global chain that, for example, implements security policies. If the processing in the global chain took place without errors, the message context is passed to the service specific chain. Handlers in this chain may manipulate the message before it is passed to the actual service. A reply message from the service is passed along a response handler chain to the client.

Axis provides a `Call` object for service invocation. After starting the invocation, the client-side message processing takes place (as shown in Figure 8.1(b)). The `Call` object contains the message context, which again is passed through the chains.

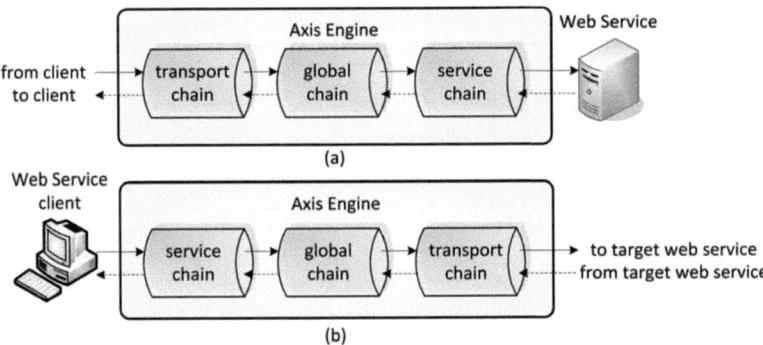

Figure 8.1: Message processing in Apache Axis (see Graham et al. [45]).

Moreover, Axis offers a serialization/deserialization mechanism that enables de-/serialization of primitive data types (e.g., `int`, `float`, etc.) and Java beans. Additionally, arrays of these types are serializable. The process of serialization and deserialization is based on the factory pattern. To realize a custom de-/serializer, the implementation of a de-/serializer factory is necessary. These factories instantiate de-/serializers for a specific class. For these classes, a so-called type mapping (a mapping between a Java class and an XML Schema type) has to be registered at the Axis type mapping registry, which can be looked up during the de-/serialization process.

8.3 XML2Java Model Generator

The XML2Java model generator creates a Java class for each XML element in an XML file. For each child element, a corresponding object is added to the class. If multiple elements of the same type occur, then a list of these objects is added instead. For each attribute, a string is added to the class with the corresponding getters and setters. For each list type, an `add()`-method is added to the class. Each created Java class furthermore contains a field `elementNamespace` to save the current namespace of the XML element and a field `elementValue` to save the string data between start and end tag. XML Namespaces are converted to Java packages. Numbers (for example, years) are preceded by an 'n' in the conversion process, since Java packages must not start with a number.

The model generator tries to build a "best practice" model. The model becomes finer the more input data it gets, i.e. it reflects the union of the structures of all XML input files. For policies that usually have a simple model, a short number of examples is sufficient to build a complete model of the policy in Java. For a very complex specification like WSDL, more files are needed. An advantage of this approach is that the model is only as complex as the files to be processed. In the case of WSDL, there are many parts of the specification, which might not be used, hence the model does not reflect these parts. For example, the `definitions` tag in all the files encountered so far has one `service` tag whereas, according to the WSDL 1.1 specification, it could contain many services. In practice, a WSDL file is only used to describe exactly one service. By only taking into account the features that are really used, the complexity of the model is reduced and hence it is easier to work with the model. A parser on top of the model can be build more easily. If the model is not sufficient for a specific WSDL file, it can simply be extended by being "trained" with the file. This approach is useful if the developer has in-depth knowledge of the XML specification. The Java representation reflects the structure of the XML files very closely and can thus be easily used.

The XML2Java model generator was used as a foundation for the implementation tasks dealing with WS-Policies, temporal policies, WSDL, and XML Schema.

8.4 Temporal Policy

In this section, a prototypical implementation of the Temporal Policy Runtime Environment is presented. The focus is laid on management and deployment of the temporal policies. Furthermore, the integration of the temporal policy into the Axis framework is described.

8.4.1 Temporal Policy Runtime Environment

The implementation of the Temporal Policy Runtime Environment consists of two central components: Repository Manager and Weaver. The `TemporalPolicyManager` acts as the Repository Manager and is implemented as a singleton. It reads all policy documents from a given folder every ten seconds. If the last modified attribute of the file changed between two consecutive reads or a policy has been added or removed, the corresponding model files are added, refreshed, or removed from the `TemporalPolicyManager`. For the temporal policies, the XML2Java model generator was used to generate a `TemporalPolicy` class with the following objects (representing the child elements of a temporal policy),

- `expires`
- `startTime`
- `endTime`
- `duration`
- `onActivation`
- `onRenewal`
- `onExpiration`
- `onDeactivation`

with the following string fields (representing the attributes)

- `name`
- `keywords`

and the standard fields `elementValue` and `elementNamespace`.

The different fields hold values for the corresponding XML elements and attributes. The `TemporalPolicyManager` additionally holds three maps. The first map `tempol2policy` takes a temporal policy as a key and returns a list of policies and temporal policies as a value. This map is used to see which temporal policies and WS-Policies are influenced by the temporal policy given as a key. The second map `policy2tempol` works the other way round. This map can be used to provide a policy as a key and get a list of temporal policies influencing the policy. The third map `service2policies` takes a service name as key and returns a list of policies associated with that service.

With the first map, the `TemporalPolicyManager` is able to add new temporal policies when

- new policies are added to the monitored folder,

8.4. Temporal Policy

- policies are activated,
- policies are renewed

or remove temporal policies when

- they expire,
- they get deactivated,
- they are removed from the monitored folder.

The second and third map are important for the `Weaver`. When a WSDL file is requested, the `Weaver` looks up the policies for the requested service in the `service2policies` map. Then, for each policy found, the Weaver checks if there is an active temporal policy for the given policy. The policy is then woven into the WSDL description of the service. Depending on the kind of policy, different concrete weavers can be used, such as a weaver for a communication policy, a weaver for a security policy, etc.

8.4.2 Integration of Policy Weaving into the Axis Framework

Whenever a service's WSDL document is requested in Axis, the WSDL document is, by default, generated on the fly. To influence the generation of the WSDL document, a handler can be registered in a process' response flow. A temporal policy handler (`TPHandler`) has been implemented to be placed in the response flow of each service. It instructs the weaver to do the lookup and, if needed, weave policies into the WSDL. Currently, the policies are woven into the WSDL document as a whole. A more fine-grained weaving process could be implemented in the future. The complete process of requesting a WSDL including the weaving is shown in Figure 8.2.

For another SOAP engine, the `TPHandler` can be easily replaced, since this is only a component acting as a "frontend" to the actual functionality.

8.4.3 Integrating the Temporal Policy Manager into a Servlet Engine

Servlet engines like Apache Tomcat and Jetty implement the Servlet specification that dictates to offer a `ServletContextListener` interface. This interface can be used to react to the start and shutdown of the servlet container. In the `web.xml` configuration file, a custom servlet context listener that starts the `TemporalPolicyManager` can be registered. When Tomcat or Jetty is started, the custom servlet context listener is executed and initializes the

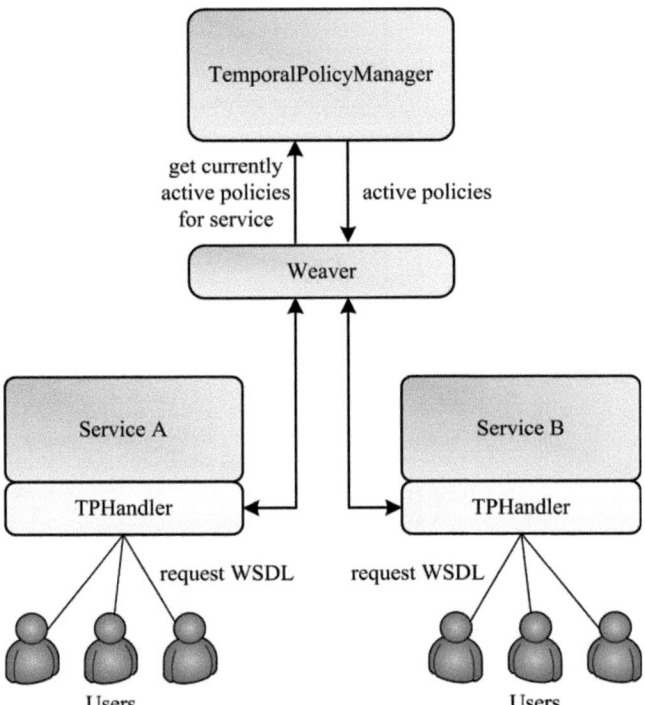

Figure 8.2: Policy weaving.

8.5. Communication Policy

TemporalPolicyManager. Listing 8.1 shows the adapted web.xml configuration file for Apache Axis that additionally registers a custom servlet context listener (de.fb12.flexswa.axis.tomcat.ServerContextListener) to be started when the Axis web application is loaded.

```
<web-app>
  <display-name>Apache-Axis</display-name>

  <listener>
    <listener-class>
      org.apache.axis.transport.http.AxisHTTPSessionListener
    </listener-class>
  </listener>
  <listener>
    <listener-class>
      de.fb12.flexswa.axis.tomcat.ServerContextListener
    </listener-class>
  </listener>

  <servlet>
    <servlet-name>AxisServlet</servlet-name>
    <display-name>Apache-Axis Servlet</display-name>
    <servlet-class>
      org.apache.axis.transport.http.AxisServlet
    </servlet-class>
  </servlet>

  ...
</web-app>
```

Listing 8.1: Modified Apache Axis web.xml.

8.4.4 Integrating the Temporal Policy Manager into the Globus Toolkit

The ServerContextListener can be reused by the Globus Toolkit. The Globus Toolkit start scripts are modified to start a custom bootstrapper instead of the Globus bootstrapper. The custom bootstrapper starts the ServerContext-Listener and the original bootstrap class.

8.5 Communication Policy

This section presents an implementation of the communication policy. Again, the XML2Java model generator is used to create a Java model of the communication policy. A *communication policy weaver* and *communication policy interpreter* have been implemented to weave the policy into the WSDL and to interpret the contents of a communication policy. The communication policy is integrated into the Axis framework and into the Globus Toolkit.

8.5.1 Communication Policy Model

The created communication policy class only contains a list of `ExactlyOne` and `All` (being the structure of each WS-Policy). More interesting is the created `ExactlyOne` class containing the following objects of type list (representing the elements of a communication policy)

- `filetransfer`
- `client`
- `protocol`
- `ExactlyOne`
- `All`

and the standard fields `elementValue` and `elementNamespace`.

For weaving, the same weaver as for temporal policies (see Section 8.4.1) can be used and thus the communication policies can be integrated into the Temporal Policy Runtime Environment.

8.5.2 Standalone Communication Policy

The communication policy can also be used standalone. Then, a simple service description can be used to associate a service with different policies (as shown in Listing 8.2).

```
<service name="VideoOnDemandService" provider="java:RPC">
  <responseFlow>
    <handler type="CommunicationPolicyHandler"/>
  </responseFlow>
  <parameter name="allowedMethods" value="*"/>
  <parameter name="className"
    value="de.fb12.flexswa.services.VideoOnDemandService"/>
  <parameter name="compols"
    value="http://fb12.de/compol/video_on_demand_policy"/>
</service>
```

Listing 8.2: Axis service description including a reference to the communication policy.

8.5. Communication Policy

To determine which policies to use for this service, standard Axis name/value-pairs are used. Whereas `allowedMethods` and `className` are standard Axis parameters, the `compols` parameter has a space separated list of communication policy names (i.e. usually URIs) as its value.

When Tomcat is started, a custom servlet context listener reads the Axis `server-config.wsdd` file. For each service, a `parameter map` is created providing a mapping between the parameter name and the parameter value. Each parameter map is put into the `service map` that again holds a mapping from a service to its parameters. To additionally allow the use of the communication policy in a WSRF-Grid, the implementation of the communication policy has been integrated into the Globus Toolkit. Since the Globus Toolkit uses a separate `server-config.wsdd` for each service, *all* `server-config.wsdd` files are read by the custom servlet context listener to build the service map.

Additionally, there is another weaver for generating simple communication policies from an Apache Axis service configuration file. Listing 8.3 shows a service description including the parameters to create a communication policy.

```
<service name="VideoOnDemandService" provider="java:RPC">
  <responseFlow>
    <handler type="CommunicationPolicyHandler"/>
  </responseFlow>
  <parameter name="allowedMethods" value="*"/>
  <parameter name="className"
    value="de.fb12.flexswa.services.VideoOnDemandService"/>
  <parameter name="protocol"
    value="RTP RTPv2 rtp://137.248.121.11:22222/video"/>
  <parameter name="filetransfer"
    value="ftp pull ftp://ftp.fb12.de -"/>
  <parameter name="client" value="- download
    http://downloads.fb12.de/VideoOnDemandClient"/>
</service>
```

Listing 8.3: Axis service description including information for the communication policy.

The parameters `protocol`, `filetransfer`, and `client` are used for the generation of the communication policy. Each parameter has a value list separated by a space character. The first token of the `protocol` list is the name of the protocol, the second the version and the third the endpoint URI. If a multiple of three tokens is provided, for every three tokens a policy alternative is generated, i.e. one child element of the `ExactlyOne` element.

The first token of the `filetransfer` list provides the name of the protocol, the second the type, the third the endpoint of the protocol, and the forth the protocol version or namespace in which the protocol is defined. Again, a multiple of four tokens results in policy alternatives.

The first token of the `client` list is the name of the client (which can be omitted by using a '-'), the second is the type of the client and the third is the URI which identifies the client (and its location). A multiple of three tokens results in policy alternatives.

To add the communication policy to the WSDL, a `CPHandler` has been implemented and added to the service chain. When the WSDL is requested, the parameter map of this service is read and the Communication Policy Interpreter fills the generated Java model. The communication policy is then generated by the weaver from the Java model and added to the WSDL description of the service on-the-fly. Then, the WSDL is returned to the requester.

The integration of the communication policy into Flex-SwA to describe streaming and file transfer protocol implementations is shown in Section 8.6.8.

8.6 Flex-SwA

This section presents the implementation of the Flex-SwA architecture based on Java 5. First, the middleware-agnostic structure of Flex-SwA is explained and then the supported protocols and de-/serialization mechanisms are described, followed by an overview of the different threads used in Flex-SwA.

8.6.1 Middleware Components

The structure of Flex-SwA has been designed for providing adaptability to other middleware technologies besides web or Grid services. As a start, an overview of the different middleware components is given, as shown in Figure 8.3.

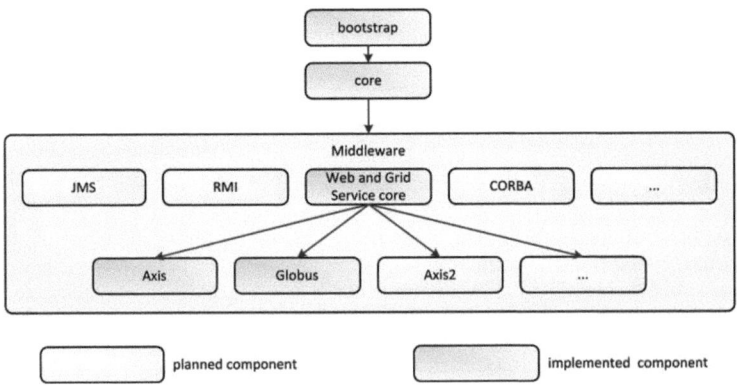

Figure 8.3: Middleware components of Flex-SwA.

8.6. Flex-SwA

The main two components of Flex-SwA are the *bootstrap* and *core* component. In the *bootstrap* component, all the classes that have to be loaded when the JVM is started are located. These classes contain the protocols that have to be registered at the `java.net.URL` class and depending on this the `Reference` (as a central class of Flex-SwA), buffers, and the `FlexSwAServer` the `Reference` class depends on and a few others. The *core* comprises all the classes that do not need to be bootstrapped but on which all further components depend, for example, most of the threads for the retrieval of the referenced data, the handling of the communication policy, the servers offered by Flex-SwA, and the service logic of the different services. On top of the *core* component, different middleware could be used, for example, `JMS`, `RMI`, `CORBA`, etc. Since Flex-SwA was originally planned to be used in service-oriented environments, the focus is laid on the implementation of the *service core* that can be adapted to specific web or Grid service engines. Two components (`Axis`, `Globus`) have actually been implemented, one for Apache Axis 1.2 RC2 (or newer) and one for the Globus Toolkit 4.0.x. The `Axis` component works with Apache Tomcat 5.5.9 (or newer) and Jetty 5.1.10 (or newer).

8.6.2 Protocol Capabilities

Figure 8.4 gives an overview of the protocols that are supported for the transfer of large amounts of data and for post-invocation parameter transmission (PIPT). For PIPT, outports and inports can be created to build an external channel and provide serialization and deserialization mechanisms.

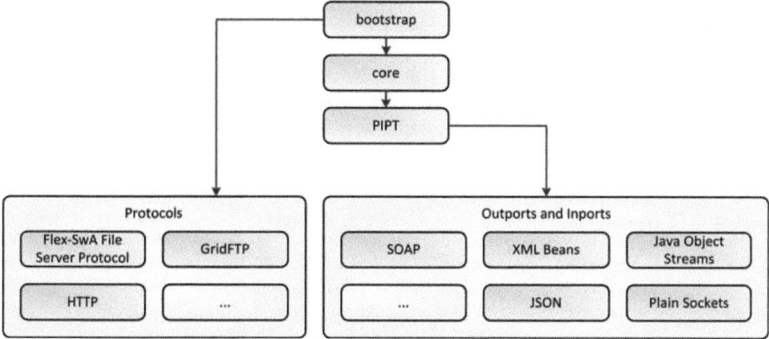

Figure 8.4: Protocol capabilities for transferring large amounts of data and PIPT.

Concretely, for large amounts of data, the `Flex-SwA File Server Protocol`, HTTP or `GridFTP` can be used. For PIPT, data can be directly streamed over `Plain Sockets`, sent per `Java Object Streams`, `JSON`, as `XML Beans`, or via

SOAP. For the `JSON` and `XML Beans` serialization, the XStream library [2] was used. For the SOAP serialization, the serializer of Apache Axis was extracted for standalone use. Listing 8.4 shows an outport that performs JSON encoding.

8.6.3 Buffers

When using PIPT, the external channel is built as soon as a consumer tries to read from an inport corresponding to the reference. To enable the producer to "send" data before the connection is established, the data is buffered. Figure 8.5 shows the buffers available in Flex-SwA.

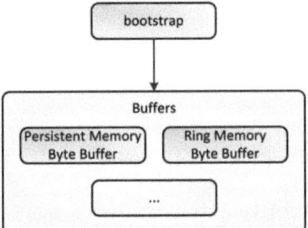

Figure 8.5: Buffers used in Flex-SwA.

For data buffering, two different buffer implementations are available: a `PersistentMemoryByteBuffer` and a `RingMemoryByteBuffer`. The persistent buffer buffers all data written to it. The buffer will overflow if more data is written to it as specified at instantiation. The ring buffer will not overflow. If the ring buffer is full, write operations to it will be blocked until data has been read from it. The advantage of the persistent buffer is that it can simply be rewound and read again. The ring buffer can only be read once, but works by only allocating small amounts of memory.

8.6.4 Threads

A few different threads can be used to handle the different communication patterns, as shown in Figure 8.6. The different threads depend on either the *bootstrap* or *core* component, respectively. The lazy nonblocking threads (`LNB Thread` and `LNB Memory Thread`) are used by the `Reference` directly (which is part of the *bootstrap* component) to acquire the data when first needed. The eager nonoverlapping concurrent and the eager overlapping threads (`ENC Thread`, `ENC Memory Thread`, `EO Thread`, and `EO Memory Thread`) are used after the deserialization process to start the data transfer eagerly, i.e. directly before the service is started. For lazy blocking and for iterative handling of the data, no thread is needed.

8.6. Flex-SwA

```
public class JSONOutport implements IOutport
{
  private boolean autoflushed = true;
  ObjectOutputStream oos;
  OutputStream os;
  XStream xstream;

  protected JSONOutport()
  {
    super();
    this.autoflushed = true;
  }

  public JSONOutport(OutputStream os) throws IOException
  {
    this();
    this.xstream = new XStream(new JettisonMappedXmlDriver());
    this.oos = xstream.createObjectOutputStream(os);
    this.os = os;
    oos.flush();
  }

  public JSONOutport(Reference ref) throws FlexSwAException,
    IOException
  {
    //request a local running memory buffer to write to
    this(ref.requestMemoryOutputStream(100 * 1024));
  }

  public void write(Object o) throws FlexSwAException
  {
    try
    {
      oos.writeObject(o);
      if (autoflushed) flush();
    }
    catch (Exception e)
    {
      throw new FlexSwAException(e);
    }
  }

  ...
}
```

Listing 8.4: Implementation of a JSON outport.

94   Implementation

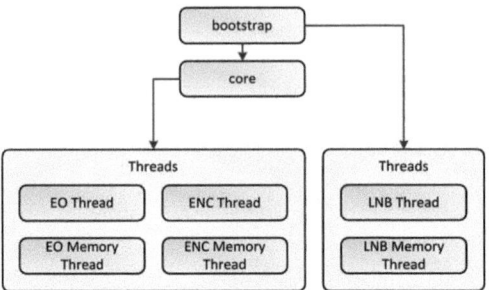

Figure 8.6: Threads used in Flex-SwA.

8.6.5 Interaction

Figure 8.7 gives a complete overview of the interaction of the different components. A web service client creates a `Flex-SwA Call` object with a specific service and operation to invoke. If a reference is used, the `Reference Serializer` creates an XML representation of the reference according to the XML Schema shown in Listing 5.2. Then, the `Axis HTTP Transport` sends the data to the target service. Listing 8.5 shows how easy the invocation of a web service using the `Flex-SwA Call` is by presenting a client for the `audio resynthesis (WebVoice) service` (see Section 9.3).

If a URL is used instead of a reference as a parameter for the Flex-SwA Call, the data is pushed to a (Flex-SwA) server according to the communication policy of the service.

At server-side, the Axis Transport receives the SOAP message and processes it. First, a `Reference Handler` is used to determine how many references the SOAP message contains. Then, the SOAP message is processed by the `Reference Deserializer` that deserializes the XML representation of the references into objects. After looking up the different modes (data transmission, service execution, concurrency, blocking mode), the `Reference Deserializer` delegates the communication to the corresponding threads or lets the service handle the communication directly.

- **Eager Nonoverlapping Iterative:** The `Reference Deserializer` acquires the data directly. References are resolved sequentially.

- **Eager Nonoverlapping Concurrent:** The `Reference Deserializer` delegates the communication to multiple eager nonoverlapping concurrent threads (`ENC Thread`) and waits for them to finish. The `ENC Threads` retrieve the data concurrently.

8.6. Flex-SwA

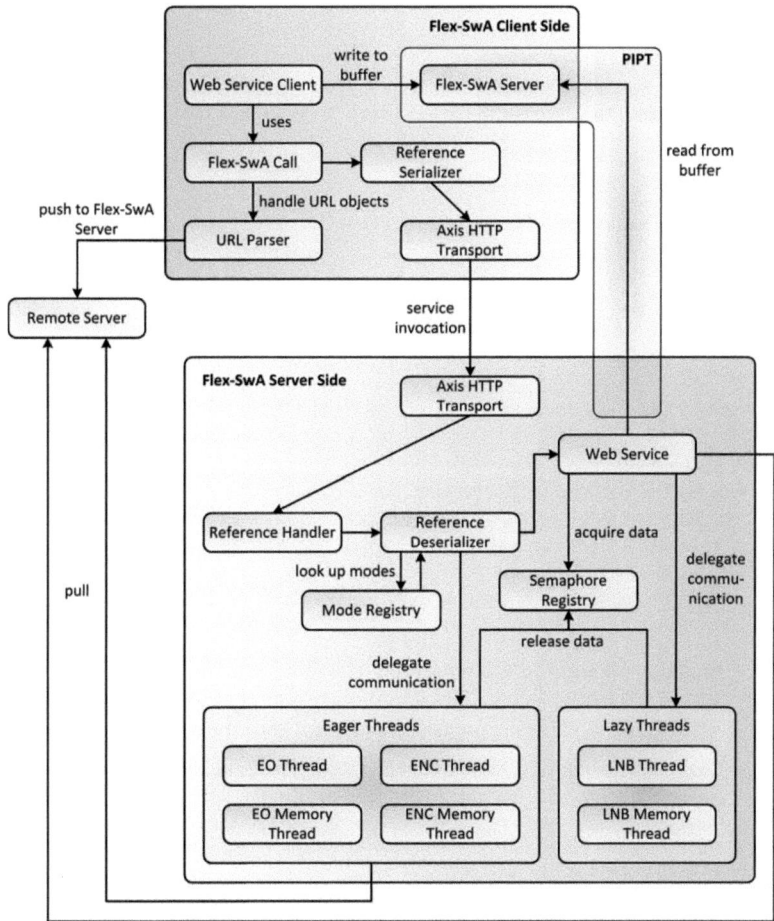

Figure 8.7: Interaction between the components of Flex-SwA.

```
public class WebVoiceClient
{
  public static void main(String[] args)
  {
    try
    {
      FlexSwACall f = new FlexSwACall(
        "http://pc12835.mathematik.uni-marburg.de" +
        ":8080/axis/services/WebVoice", "wav2splice");
      Reference ref = new Reference();
      ref.requestHostingURL("SA1.WAV", false);
      Reference ret = (Reference)
        f.invoke(new Object[]{ref, false, 12, 0, 0.5, 4.0, 30});
      System.out.println(ret.getResourceUrl());
    }
    catch(Exception e)
    {
      e.printStackTrace();
    }
  }
}
```

Listing 8.5: `WebVoice` client using the `Flex-SwA` Call.

- **Eager Overlapping Iterative:** For each reference, a `Job` object is added to an eager overlapping thread (`EO Thread`) that is started at the end of the `Reference Deserializer` that resolves the references one after another. Directly after the thread is started, the execution is given back to the Axis Engine. As soon as the job is finished, the data is released for the service to access.

- **Eager Overlapping Concurrent:** The same as Eager Overlapping Iterative. Instead of resolving the references one after another, the references are resolved in parallel.

- **Lazy Nonblocking:** The `Reference Deserializer` does not handle references in a special manner and the Axis Engine proceeds. The service itself can use the `Reference` object to retrieve the referenced data by calling the `acquire()` method that delegates the communication to the lazy nonblocking thread (`LNB Thread`). The `LNB Thread` then retrieves the referenced data and releases the lock for the data, such that the service can access it.

- **Lazy Blocking:** The `Reference Deserializer` does not handle references in a special manner and the Axis Engine proceeds. The service itself uses the `Reference` object to acquire the referenced data. While the data is transferred, the execution of the service blocks.

If the *memory mode* is specified to keep the referenced data in memory, the corresponding memory threads are used instead.

To realize PIPT, the client requests memory for a local buffer at a local running Flex-SwA server instance and writes data to the buffer—either before or after the service invocation. The buffer can then be read over the network by a specific inport (see Figure 8.4). Listing 8.6 shows an inport that handles JSON decoding (corresponding to Listing 8.4).

8.6.6 Configuration of the Web Service Container

The Flex-SwA configuration for a web service container can be done by using the configuration file `flexswa.properties`. This properties file defines parameters as name-value pairs to determine the behaviour of Flex-SwA. Listing 8.7 shows an example of a properties file.

SERVER_CONFIG_WSDD determines the path to the `server-config.wsdd` to which the Flex-SwA configuration has been deployed to. PATH_TO_WEBAPP is the directory where the web application resides, normally Axis. SERVER is used to list the servers that shall be started by the custom `ServletContextListener`. The first part is the (fully-qualified) class name that should be instantiated. The second part (behind the colon) is the port the server listens to. If multiple servers are to be run, the servers are simply listed as shown in Listing 8.8.

Furthermore, a `ReferenceHandler` and type mappings for Reference and Credential are added to the global Axis configuration.

8.6.7 Deploying a Flex-SwA Service

To deploy a Flex-SwA service, a few additions have to be made to the deployment descriptor of a service. Listing 8.9 shows a typical deployment descriptor. The Flex-SwA additions are the four parameters specifying the modes and the handler entries. The `ReferenceHandler` is added to the handler chain of the service. Different parameters are set for the service analog to the communication patterns described in Section 5.3.3. The `WSDLHandler` adds a communication policy to the WSDL description of a service upon access. If the additions are not provided, the globally defined transmission, processing, blocking, concurrency, and memory modes of the platform are used.

8.6.8 Communication Policy Support in Flex-SwA

Flex-SwA offers the use of the communication policy to describe the protocols services rely on for streaming as well as file transfers. The protocols and the corresponding namespaces Flex-SwA offers implementations for are shown in Table 8.1.

```java
public class JSONInport implements IInport
{
  XStream xstream;
  ObjectInputStream ois;
  InputStream is;

  public JSONInport(InputStream is) throws IOException
  {
    this.xstream = new XStream(new JettisonMappedXmlDriver());
    this.ois = xstream.createObjectInputStream(is);
    this.is = is;
  }

  public JSONInport(Reference ref) throws ConnectorException
    , IOException
  {
    //retrieve an InputStream (to read data from the network)
    this(ref.retrieveInputStream());
  }

  public void close() throws IOException
  {
    ois.close();
    try
    {
      is.close();
    }
    catch (Exception e)
    {
      e.printStackTrace();
    }
  }

  public Object read() throws FlexSwAException
  {
    try
    {
      return ois.readObject();
    }
    catch (Exception e)
    {
      throw new FlexSwAException(e);
    }
  }
}
```

Listing 8.6: Implementation of a JSON inport.

8.6. Flex-SwA

```
SERVER_CONFIG_WSDD=
  %WEBSERVER_HOME%/webapps/axis/WEB-INF/server-config.wsdd
PATH_TO_WEBAPP=%WEBSERVER_HOME%/webapps/axis/
SERVER=de.fb12.flexswa.infrastructure.servers.FlexSwAServer:8091
```
Listing 8.7: Example `flexswa.properties` file.

```
...
SERVER=de.fb12.flexswa.infrastructure.servers.FlexSwAServer:8091
SERVER=com.bar.servers.HttpServer:8092
SERVER=de.foo.servers.GridFTPServer:8093
...
```
Listing 8.8: Running multiple servers.

```xml
<deployment
  xmlns="http://xml.apache.org/axis/wsdd/"
  xmlns:java="http://xml.apache.org/axis/wsdd/providers/java">
  <service name="ENCService" provider="java:RPC">
    <parameter name="className"
      value="de.fb12.flexswa.services.ReferenceService"/>
    <parameter name="allowedMethods" value="*"/>
    <parameter name="transmissionMode" value="EAGER"/>
    <parameter name="processingMode" value="NONOVERLAPPING"/>
    <parameter name="concurrencyMode" value="CONCURRENT"/>
    <parameter name="memoryMode" value="FILE"/>
    <requestFlow>
      <handler type="ReferenceHandler"/>
    </requestFlow>
    <responseFlow>
      <handler type="WSDLHandler"/>
    </responseFlow>
  </service>
</deployment>
```
Listing 8.9: Example of a deployment descriptor for Flex-SwA.

Table 8.1: Protocols supported by Flex-SwA and their corresponding namespaces.

File transfer protocol	Namespace
Flex-Swa File Server protocol	http://fb12.de/flexswa/filetransfer/2008/11/

Streaming protocol	Namespace
Plain Sockets	http://fb12.de/flexswa/pipt/2008/11/plain
Java Object Stream	http://fb12.de/flexswa/pipt/2008/11/javaobjects
XML Beans	http://fb12.de/flexswa/pipt/2008/11/xstream/xmlbeans
JSON	http://fb12.de/flexswa/pipt/2008/11/xstream/json
SOAP 1.1	http://schemas.xmlsoap.org/soap/envelope/

Furthermore, Flex-SwA is able to leverage the protocols implemented by Sun's URL class, namely HTTP and HTTPS, for example.

8.7 Web and Grid Service Browser

This section describes the implementation of the Web and Grid Service Browser. There are several aspects to take into account when choosing the right technologies for an implementation of the Web and Grid Service Browser.

A web or Grid service user needs a familiar environment to work with services. This can be achieved by extending a popular web browser like Microsoft Internet Explorer or Mozilla Firefox. Both web browsers offer extension points to add functionality to them. Since the Internet Explorer can only be used on Windows operating systems, Mozilla Firefox was chosen to be extended by an add-on/plugin.

Generally, to extend Firefox' functionality

- an overlay for parts of the browser can be defined in the XML User Interface Language (XUL) and the additional functionality can be provided by JavaScript functions,

- a Cross Platform Component Object Model (XPCOM) component—handling the registration process of the add-on and the event processing taking place before the GUI of the browser is loaded—can be written in JavaScript or C++.

To avoid a complete reimplementation of a web/Grid service stack, it is desirable to use an existing widespread SOAP engine that can be used in conjunction

8.7. Web and Grid Service Browser

with the Firefox add-on. Since the Globus Toolkit is the most popular Grid middleware for Grid services at present, an interconnection between the add-on development in JavaScript (or C++) and the existing middleware code written in Java will be tried with the goal to reimplement as few existing features as possible.

Since Firefox offers the capability to use custom search engines, a search engine for finding web and Grid services can be directly added to the browser's search engines. This way, a user can easily search for services without having to use unaccustomed search engines that mainly find *normal* search results and only rarely web or Grid services.

To allow an easy to use interface for the user, several mechanisms (as well as the combinations of these) are possible.

- Creation of a browser overlay with XUL and JavaScript.

- Creation of new windows with input fields (again by using XUL and JavaScript).

- Using HTML forms with the advantage of providing a very familiar look to the user.

8.7.1 Firefox Add-on

The Web and Grid Service Browser is designed as a Firefox add-on working with Firefox 2 and Firefox 3.

Two XPCOM components have been developed. The first one is an *observer*, the second one a *stream converter*. The first goal is to enable Firefox to show the user a generated web page with input fields instead of the WSDL file the user clicked on. Therefore, the `http-on-examine-response` topic has to be observed. It allows to change the content type of the received document to a custom content type for which the stream converter is registered. To make the observer work correctly, it has to be registered at the observer service. However, it is not sufficient to register the observer at the service in the registering process of the XPCOM component, since this process only takes place when the add-on is installed or when changes to other add-ons occur. Hence, when Firefox starts the next time, the observer is no longer registered at the observer service.

The correct registering process is more complex. The observer has to subscribe to the `xpcom-startup` topic. To make the subscription persistent, the subscription is done by adding a category entry to the category manager during the registration process of the add-on (i.e. when the add-on is installed). After the registration, the `observe` function of the observer is called whenever the XPCOM component is loaded, which happens whenever Firefox is started, but before the browser window(s) is/are opened. In the `observe` function, the topic is checked. If the topic is `xpcom-startup`, then the topics `http-on-examine-response` and http-on-modify-request are registered with the observer service. Now, whenever a HTTP response arrives, the content type can be changed from text/xml to text/mywsdl; text/mywsdl is a custom content type for which the stream converter component is called. Listing 8.10 shows the structure of the observe function.

```
observe: function(subject,topic,data)
{
  if (topic == "xpcom-startup")
  {
    var observerService = Components
      .classes["@mozilla.org/observer-service;1"]
      .getService(Components.interfaces.nsIObserverService);
    observerService.addObserver(this,
      "http-on-examine-response", false);
    observerService.addObserver(this,
      "http-on-modify-request", false);
  }
  else if (topic == "http-on-examine-response")
  {
    //check if HTTP response is a WSDL message
    ...
  }
  else if (topic == "http-on-modify-request")
  {
    ...
  }
  ...
}
```

Listing 8.10: Structure of the observe function.

The stream converter is an XPCOM component that is registered at the category manager. The stream converter essentially offers three functions: onStartRequest, onDataAvailable, and onStopRequest. When the actual remote web page is downloaded, onStartRequest is called. In this function, the content type is changed to */* to make Firefox process the result of the stream converter normally. The onDataAvailable function is called when data from the remote web page is available for processing. In this function, a (scriptable) input stream is opened and the data from the remote web page is saved as a string. In the onStopRequest function, the processing of the completely downloaded document starts. If the document is a WSDL document, user interface generation will take place. The document will be replaced by an HTML page that contains HTML forms for the corresponding fields in the WSDL description. Listing 8.11 shows the structure of the stream converter.

The generation of the HTML page is done in Java. The advantage of this approach is that the generation can be triggered remotely by sending an XMLHttp-

8.7. Web and Grid Service Browser

```
function WSDLStreamConverter ()
{
}

...

WSDLStreamConverter.prototype.onStartRequest =
  function (aRequest, aContext)
{
  this.sourcedata = ""; //initialize buffer for web site
  //retrieve URL
  this.uri = aRequest
    .QueryInterface(Components.interfaces.nsIChannel).URI.spec;
  this.charset = aRequest
    .QueryInterface(Components.interfaces.nsIChannel)
    .contentCharset;
  this.channel = aRequest;
  //contentType */* tells Firefox to decide what to do next
  //with the stream
  this.channel.contentType ="*/*";
  this.channel.contentCharset = "UTF-8";
  this.listener.onStartRequest (this.channel, aContext);
};

WSDLStreamConverter.prototype.onDataAvailable =
  function (aRequest, aContext, aInputStream, aOffset, aCount)
{
  //buffer web site completely
  var si = Components
    .classes["@mozilla.org/scriptableinputstream;1"]
    .createInstance();
  si = si.QueryInterface(Components.interfaces
                         .nsIScriptableInputStream);
  si.init(aInputStream);
  this.sourcedata += si.read (aCount);
}

WSDLStreamConverter.prototype.onStopRequest =
  function (aRequest, aContext, aStatusCode)
{
  //generate HTML site
  //replace WSDL with generated HTML site
  ...
}
```

Listing 8.11: Structure of the **stream converter** component.

Request to a Java servlet or locally by directly calling the generate() method. Since the re-use of an available SOAP engine like Apache Axis or a Grid middleware like the Globus Toolkit was intended, a bridge from Firefox to Java is needed anyway.

8.7.2 Java Bridge

To enable Firefox to execute Java code, the Java Firefox Extension from the SIMILE project [71] was adapted from Firefox 1 to Firefox 3 and then used as a third XPCOM component. The extension uses LiveConnect to execute Java code from JavaScript. The extension loads all the Globus libraries and the self-written libraries and classes. It offers to generate an object by calling a classes' constructor, to call an object's method, or write to or read from an object's field. Even static methods are supported. The Java Bridge is implemented as a singleton, added to the category manager upon registration and can be requested as a service. Thus, the Java Bridge can be obtained from anywhere in the add-on and Java code can be executed from there. To initialize the Java Bridge, a browser overlay is needed, since a reference to the loaded Java runtime can be obtained from there.

8.7.3 Browser Overlay

Firefox offers the opportunity to overlay elements of the browser with newly defined elements. This overlay code is executed directly after the code of the overlayed element has been executed. This mechanism can be used to execute code directly after the browser's main window has opened. At this particular time, the Java Bridge is initialized as shown in Listing 8.12.

An overlay does not only provide the opportunity to run initialization code but also overlay elements. Thus, an overlay was used to provide an *Options* menu, where the user can enter URLs for the user interface generator, the execution engine, the result presentation engine and the location of certificates for the Globus Toolkit.

8.7.4 User Interface Generation

With a bridge to Java available, when the document in the onStopRequest method is really a WSDL document, it is possible to generate a user interface locally or remotely. The interface can, for example, be based on HTML forms, but it is also possible to select different (remote) user interface generators offering a more sophisticated UI. The generator returns a string containing the HTML page with JavaScript and some HTML forms. A communication policy describing that one of the Flex-SwA protocols is used combined with a Flex-SwA *Reference* type in the WSDL indicates a bulk data transfer. For each *Reference*, a file input

8.7. Web and Grid Service Browser

```
//prints messages to the error console
function console(msg)
{
    Components.classes["@mozilla.org/consoleservice;1"]
      .getService(Components.interfaces.nsIConsoleService)
      .logStringMessage(msg);
}

//initialize Java Bridge
var javabridge = Components
  .classes["@de.fb12.gridbrowser/java-bridge;1"]
  .getService(Components.interfaces.nsIJavaBridge);
if (!javabridge.wrappedJSObject.initialize(java, true))
{
    console(javabridge.wrappedJSObject.error);
}
...
```

Listing 8.12: Initialization of the Java Bridge.

that allows the selection of the file to transfer is generated. The actual transfer is started by the service pulling the bulk data from the referenced node.

JavaScript allows the user to select the port and port type to use, the operation to invoke, and assists the user in selecting which type to use for a message part. All inputs are collected when the user clicks the invoke button, and put into a SOAP message which is transmitted via an XMLHttpRequest to an execution engine. For this purpose, some of the SOAP functionality of the SOAP engine was rebuilt in JavaScript. This has the advantage that no further encoding is needed and the SOAP body can be reused in the execution engine and does not need to be generated from encoded input field values.

The use of an XMLHttpRequest indicates that the execution engine is executed remotely. This is possible, but not necessary. If the execution engine is executed remotely, the result is presented as usual. For local execution, the third topic the observer subscribed to comes into play. The http-on-modify-request allows the observer to change an HTTP request before Firefox sends it to the remote site. If local processing is desired, Firefox' capability to cancel the current request is used and the execution engine is started using the Java Bridge. In Firefox 2, the request is still executed but the response is dropped. This behaviour is sufficient most of the time. In Firefox 3, the request is directly canceled.

Unfortunately, Firefox provides no means to return a result from the observe function where the canceling of the request is realized. Thus, a way to return the result to the browser is needed. This can be done by identifying the tab that made the XMLHttpRequest and change its content. To achieve this, several steps are executed the first time a document is identified as a WSDL document in the *onStopRequest* method: First, an attribute named gridbrowser-tab is assigned to each already opened tab with a consecutive number as its value. Second, three event listeners are added to the tab container for the events `TabOpen`, `TabMove`, and `TabClose`. At the moment, only the `TabOpen` listener is used, adding the `gridbrowser-tab` with a consecutive number to each newly created tab. This guarantees that each tab has an associated number that cannot be altered by moving or closing existing tabs or opening new tabs. Listing 8.13 shows how an identifier is assigned to each existing and newly created tab.

Right before generation of the client, the stream converter retrieves the current tab by requesting a reference to the window mediator's most recent window. The associated `gridbrowser-tab` number is then given to the user interface generator that adds the tab number to the generated code of the `XMLHttpRequest`'s request headers. When the user clicks the invoke button and the `XMLHttpRequest` is sent, it possesses a request header with a reference to the tab that sent it. This tab number can then be obtained by the observer from the HTTP request when it reacts to the `http-on-modify-request`. When the execution engine returns the result of the service invocation, this result can be shown in the `result` section of the referenced tab.

8.7.5 Search Engine

Since a user might want to search Grid services directly, a simple Grid service search engine has been developed that queries the Monitoring and Discovery System (MDS) of a preconfigured set of Grid nodes. The search engine can only be used remotely. It is automatically added when Firefox is started for the first time after the add-on has been installed. For this purpose, the sidebar's `addSearchEngine` function is executed in the browser overlay's initialization code, and then persisted as a preference.

The search engine itself is implemented as a Java servlet. It uses the batch script `wsrf-query` from the Globus location to query a set of Grid nodes as shown in Listing 8.14.

The parameter `-s` specifies the service URL. The return value of such a query may look the following way (as shown in Listing 8.15).

The `Entry` element describes an service entry. The child element `ServiceGroupEntryEPR` contains the address of the service group and the name of the service. The child element `MemberServiceEPR` contains the location of a member of the group.

The information contained in the WSRF-Query return message is saved into a local running Grimoires repository (see http://twiki.grimoires.org/bin/view/Grimoires/). The UI of the search engine also allows to rate services, save tags, descriptions etc. in the Grimoires repository. Figure 8.8 shows the user interface of the search engine. Figure 8.9 shows a returned search result.

8.7. Web and Grid Service Browser

```
var gb_tabCounter = 0;

function initializeBrowser()
{
  ...
  //iterate over all tabs of a browser window
  var num = browserWindow.getBrowser().browsers.length;
  for (var i = 0; i < num; i++)
  {
    var browser = browserWindow.getBrowser()
      .getBrowserAtIndex(i);
    try
    {
      //set the gridbrowser-tab attribute
      //with a consecutive number
      browser.setAttribute("gridbrowser-tab", "" + gb_tabCounter);
      gb_tabCounter++;
    }
    catch(e)
    {
      console("setting of gridbrowser-tab attribute failed" + e);
    }
  }

  //add tab listeners
  var container = browserWindow.getBrowser().tabContainer;
  container.addEventListener("TabOpen", tabAddedListener, false);
  container.addEventListener("TabMove", tabMoveListener, false);
  container.addEventListener("TabClose", tabRemovedListener,
    false);
}

function tabAddedListener(event)
{
  // newTab is the XUL element of the browser that's been added
  var newTab = event.target.linkedBrowser;
  //set the gridbrowser-tab attribute for each new tab
  //with a consecutive number
  newTab.setAttribute("gridbrowser-tab", "" + gb_tabCounter);
  gb_tabCounter++;
}
```

Listing 8.13: Assigning an identifier to each browser tab.

```
Process p = Runtime.getRuntime().exec("cmd /C "
  + this.globusLocation + "/bin/wsrf-query -s "
  + target + " > " + filepath);
```

Listing 8.14: Executing a WSRF-query from Java.

```
<ns1:Entry>
 <ns1:ServiceGroupEntryEPR>
  <ns2:Address>
   https://gt4.dgrid.hlrs.de:8443/.../ContainerRegistryEntryService
  </ns2:Address>
  <ns3:ReferenceProperties>
   <ns4:ServiceName>SecureCounterService</ns4:ServiceName>
  </ns3:ReferenceProperties>
  <ns5:ReferenceParameters />
 </ns1:ServiceGroupEntryEPR>
 <ns1:MemberServiceEPR>
  <ns6:Address>
   https://gt4.dgrid.hlrs.de:8443/.../SecureCounterService
  </ns6:Address>
  <ns7:ReferenceParameters/>
 </ns1:MemberServiceEPR>
</ns1:Entry>
```

Listing 8.15: Return Message for a WSRF-Query (namespaces left out).

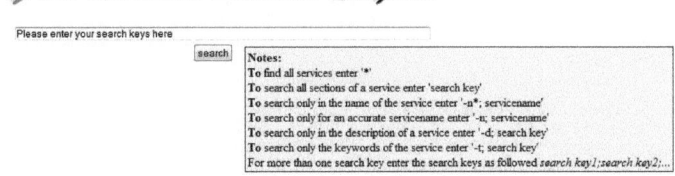

Figure 8.8: User interface of the search engine.

8.7. Web and Grid Service Browser

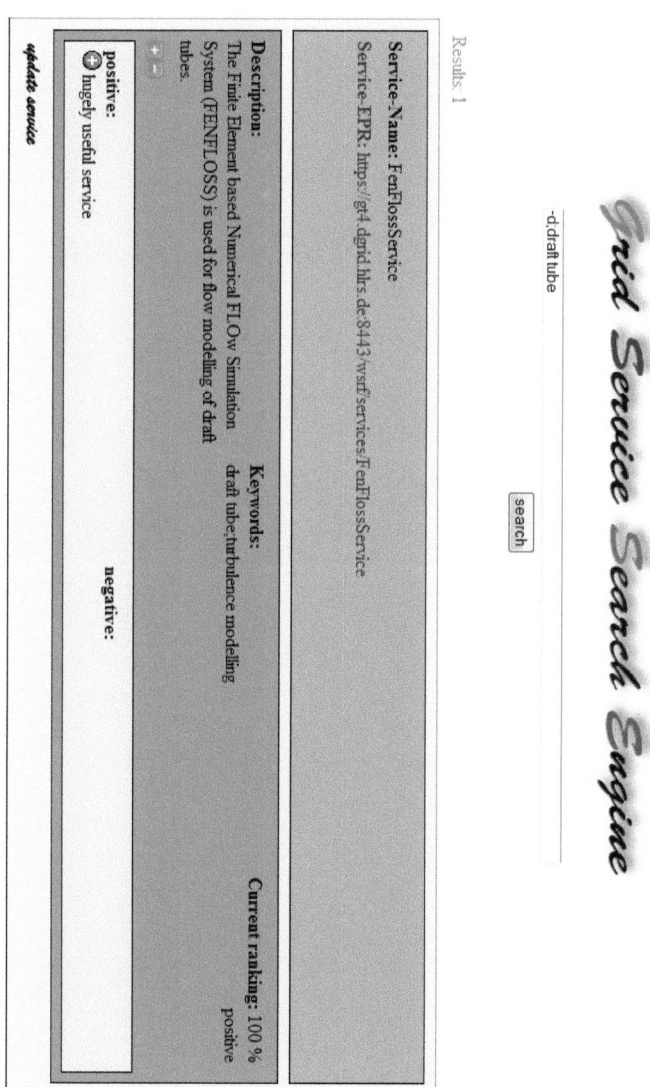

Figure 8.9: Result of a Grid service search.

8.7.6 WSDL and XML Schema Parser

The UI generator needs a WSDL parser to parse the WSDL description of web and Grid services and an XML Schema (XSD) parser for the `types` section of the WSDL document. For this purpose, a parser combining the WSDL and XML Schema parsing has been implemented on top of the XML2Java model generator. The `definitions` tag, for example, is translated into a Java class containing

- a `message` list,
- a `portType` list,
- a `binding` list,
- an `import` list,
- a `types` object, and
- a `service` object

for the child elements of the `definitions` tag and

- a `name` object and
- a `targetNamespace` object

for the attributes. Furthermore, there are two objects containing the text of the element and the namespace.

At present, the model is "trained" by some example WSDL and XSD files of the W3C, of Globus, of Axis, of Axis2, and of the .NET framework. With the parser being implemented on top of the model, it is quite easy to use the structure of the created Java classes, since it is similar to the structure of the WSDL and XSD files.

8.7.7 HTML Structure

For the graphical presentation, an HTML page working without server-side components was generated. Therefore, the necessary parts of the model information have to be reflected in the automatically generated HTML page. The creation of the SOAP body has been completely reimplemented in JavaScript and embedded into the HTML page, such that it can be used directly from the generated user interface. For each operation in each port type, a `div` container is added to the HTML page, holding a `span` for each variable. The `id` attribute of a `span` describes which of the data belongs together, as can be seen in Listing 8.16 showing the schematic HTML representation for the `wav2splice` operation of the `WebVoice` web service (see Section 9.3).

8.7. Web and Grid Service Browser

```
<div id="divop0.0" ...">...
  <span id="0:ref" class="http://core.flexswa.fb12.de"></span>
  <span id="0:ref:resourceUrl"
    class="http://core.flexswa.fb12.de">
    <input id="input1" type="file">
  </span>
  <span id="0:preservedBlockSize" class="...">
    <img src="..." onmouseover="showTooltip(...)"
      onmouseout="hideTooltip()">
    <input onmouseover="showInputTooltip(...)"
      onmouseout="hideTooltip()" value="12" type="text">
  </span>
  <span id="0:intermediateFrameCount" class="...">
    <img src="..." onmouseover="showTooltip(...)"
      onmouseout="hideTooltip()">
    <input onmouseover="showInputTooltip(...)"
      onmouseout="hideTooltip()" value="5" type="text">
  </span>
  <span id="0:steepness" class="...">
    <img src="..." onmouseover="showTooltip(...)"
      onmouseout="hideTooltip()">
    <input onmouseover="showInputTooltip(...)"
      onmouseout="hideTooltip()" value="0.5" type="text">
  </span>
  <span id="0:olaErrorTarget" class="...">
    <img src="..." onmouseover="showTooltip(...)"
      onmouseout="hideTooltip()">
    <input onmouseover="showInputTooltip(...)"
      onmouseout="hideTooltip()" value="4.0" type="text">
  </span>
  <span id="0:olaMaxIterationCount" class="...">
    <img src="..." onmouseover="showTooltip(...)"
      onmouseout="hideTooltip()">
    <input onmouseover="showInputTooltip(...)"
      onmouseout="hideTooltip()" value="150" type="text">
  </span>
</div>
```

Listing 8.16: Schematic representation of the `wav2splice` operation.

The first `span` defines an element named `ref`. The `class` attribute is used to represent the namespace of the `ref` element, namely `http://core.flex-swa.fb12.de`. The next `span` defines an element `ref:resourceUrl` that indicates that the `resourceUrl` element is part of the `ref` element. The other elements (`preservedBlockSize`, etc.) are top-level elements just like the `ref` element.

Dependent on the binding style, the SOAP message is created from the field information the user entered.

8.7.8 Proxy Certificate Generation and Execution Engine

When invoking a Grid service, a part of the form contains possible security settings. Here, GSI Transport, GSI Secure Message, and GSI Secure Conversation are supported. The user needs to have a valid certificate in a folder configured in the *Options* menu. It is also possible to use the certificate from the security device. The user then has to additionally enter the password for the security device. If no valid proxy certificate is found, one is created programmatically by the execution engine (if running locally). The execution engine is responsible for the resource creation and the correct configuration of the Axis' `Call`-object, which includes settings of the service's endpoint, operation, the service credentials, and security parameters. When Secure Message is used, the user needs to put the host certificate into his or her certificate folder by hand.

8.7.9 Result Presentation Engine

For the result presentation, different plugins can be implemented. Currently, the result presentation engine visualizes textual information, the original SOAP message, and takes care of multimedia data. Whenever bulk data is part of the service's result, the service can use Flex-SwA references to refer to the bulk data and assign a MIME type to them. Depending on the MIME type, different result presentations are used. For the MIME types `audio/x-wav` and `audio/mpeg`, an audio plugin has been implemented as part of the extension that embeds a player for and a download link to the referenced audio files into a new section of the HTML page. For the MIME types `image/png` and `image/jpeg`, a new section with previews of the pictures is created.

8.8 Service-enabled Mashup Editor

The Service-enabled Mashup Editor has been implemented as a Rich Internet Application (RIA) with the Adobe Flex SDK and the Adobe Flex Builder (being an Eclipse rich client). Adobe Flex 3 combines ActionScript 3 (used for Flash applications) and MXML used to declaratively define user interfaces with XML. An Adobe Flex application is compiled to a .swf file that can be executed by the

8.8. Service-enabled Mashup Editor 113

Adobe Flash Player from the browser. The Flash Player is available for all major operating systems (Windows, MacOS X, Linux, Solaris) and browsers (Internet Explorer, Firefox, Safari, Seamonkey, Mozilla, Netscape) and is therefore well suited to build "platform-independent" RIAs.

Figure 8.10 provides an overview of the Service-enabled Mashup Editor.

The upper left rectangle shows the *components* a user or developer is able to select for his/her application. The components are divided into different areas. There are components for image processing, video processing, audio processing, and general services.

The right rectangle shows the editor's *working area*, which is implemented by a canvas.

The lower left rectangle shows a button to switch between *views* (user and developer).

Listing 8.17 shows the MXML code to define the layout of the overview.

The editor consists of a horizontal box containing a vertical box and a canvas. The vertical box is again divided into several panels for the different service types, a horizontal box containing the button to switch between user and developer view, and a spacer that takes the space between the panels and the horizontal box at the bottom. The panels hold different (self-defined) labels representing the actual services and web applications.

8.8.1 Extensibility

The Drag&Drop handlers of the canvas actually instantiate the components when they are drawn onto the canvas, as shown in Listing 8.18.

When a component (actually the self-defined label) is "dropped" onto the canvas, then the corresponding component is instantiated and placed at the location it has been dragged to. New components can be easily added to the editor by adding another `else if` branch. The `MEAbstractComponent` is a self-defined component that offers certain Drag&Drop functionality and resizing. Furthermore, it provides functions (that have to be implemented by subcomponents) for requesting a service, querying the results, and querying inputs and outputs of the component.

8.8.2 Developer and User View

Flex allows the definition of different states for an application. It is possible to define states that are based on an already defined state or the basic state of an application. With state transitions, modifications to the UI can be defined. In Listing 8.19 the state for the developer view named `devState` and the corresponding state transition are shown.

The state transition defines the current canvas to be removed and a new canvas to be added after the main vertical box. On the new canvas, developer

Figure 8.10: Screenshot of the Service-enabled Mashup Editor.

8.8. Service-enabled Mashup Editor

```
<mx:HBox width="100%" height="100%"
    horizontalGap="25"
    id="mainHBox">
  <mx:VBox width="200" height="100%"
      id="mainVBox">
    <mx:Panel title="Image Services"
        width="100%"
        layout="vertical">
      <mash:MEAbstractLabel title="{webAppFlickr}" />
      <mash:MEAbstractLabel title="{wsFaceDetector}" />
    </mx:Panel>
    <mx:Panel title="Video Services"
        width="100%"
        layout="vertical">
      <mash:MEAbstractLabel title="{webAppYouTube}" />
      <mash:MEAbstractLabel title="{webAppFLVPlayer}" />
    </mx:Panel>
    <mx:Panel title="Audio Services"
        width="100%"
        layout="vertical">
      <mash:MEAbstractLabel title="{wsAudioService}" />
    </mx:Panel>
    <mx:Panel title="General Services"
        width="100%"
        layout="vertical">
      <mash:MEAbstractLabel title="{uploadService}" />
    </mx:Panel>
    <mx:Spacer height="100%"/>
    <mx:HBox>
      <mx:Button id="viewButton"
          icon="{bulbImage}"
          width="25"
          mouseDown="changeButtonPicture(event)"/>
    </mx:HBox>
  </mx:VBox>
  <mx:Canvas id="canvas"
      width="100%" height="100%"
      backgroundColor="0xf2f2ff"
      dragEnter="canvas_dragEnter(event);"
      dragDrop="canvas_dragDrop(event);">
    <mx:Image id="trash"
        source="{trashImage}"
        toolTip="Trash"
        dragEnter="trash_dragEnterHandler(event);"
        dragDrop="trash_dragDropHandler(event);" />
  </mx:Canvas>
</mx:HBox>
```
Listing 8.17: Definition of the editor layout.

```
private function canvas_dragDrop(event:DragEvent):void
{
  var dropTarget:Canvas=Canvas(event.currentTarget);
  ...
  var abstract:MEAbstractComponent;
  if (p.title==webAppFlickr) abstract = new FlickrComponent();
  else if (p.title==wsFaceDetector)
    abstract = new ImageFaceDetector();
  else if (p.title==webAppYouTube)
    abstract = new YouTubeComponent();
  else if (p.title==webAppFLVPlayer)
    abstract = new FLVPlayer();
  else if (p.title==uploadService)
    abstract = new UploadServiceComponent();
  //add new components here

  abstract.x = event.localX;
  abstract.y = event.localY;
  components.addItem(abstract);
  dropTarget.addChild(abstract);
}
```

Listing 8.18: Placing components on the canvas.

```
<mx:states>
  <mx:State name="devState">
    <mx:RemoveChild target="{canvas}" />
    <mx:AddChild relativeTo="{mainVBox}" position="after">
      <mx:Canvas id="devCanvas"
        width="100%" height="100%"
        backgroundColor="0xf2f2ff"
        dragEnter="canvas_dragEnter(event);"
        dragDrop="canvas_dragDrop(event);">
        ...
      </mx:Canvas>
    </mx:AddChild>
  </mx:State>
</mx:states>
```

Listing 8.19: Switching from user view to developer view.

components can be placed, whereas the old canvas holds the user components. The transition back from developer state to user state or basic state, respectively, does not need to be explicitly defined. Flex undoes the changes to the UI automatically, when the state is switched back.

8.8.3 Proxy

The Flash Player only allows a connection to a remote web server when the web server offers a `crossdomain.xml` file in which it explicitly allows connections from other computers. By default, the Flash Player tries to obtain the `crossdomain.xml` file from the root directory of the destination web server, i.e. for the domain `example.com` the default address of the `crossdomain.xml` file is http://www.example.com/crossdomain.xml.

If the destination server does not offer a `crossdomain.xml` file that allows access from the Flash Player, a proxy is needed. To host the mashup editor and the proxy, Apache Tomcat is used. To use the proxy, Tomcat itself needs a `crossdomain.xml` file that it hosts as as a root file. This can be achieved by placing the `crossdomain.xml` file in the `ROOT` web application folder of Tomcat.

The proxy is implemented as a Java servlet that realizes downloads and web service invocations. The proxy is used whenever a direct use of services is not possible. Furthermore, the proxy is used for Grid service invocations. To invoke Grid services, the capabilities of the Web and Grid Service Browser—more precisely the execution engine—is used.

8.9 Summary

This chapter has presented the realization of the temporal and communication policy and the implementation of the Flex-SwA architecture, the Web and Grid Service Browser, and the Service-enabled Mashup Editor. To use temporal policies, a Temporal Policy Runtime Environment, consisting of a Temporal Policy Manager and a Policy Weaver, has been implemented. The Temporal Policy Manager maintains all the policies: It adds new policies and removes expired ones. The Policy Weaver weaves active policies directly into a requested WSDL document upon request. In this way, also active communication policies can be woven into the WSDL. To use communication policies, a communication policy interpreter has been implemented to be used on client-side to interpret the protocols a communication policy describes. Both policies can be integrated into the Apache Axis framework.

The implementation of the Flex-SwA architecture shows the modular concept via which Flex-SwA can also be implemented for other middleware technologies than web and Grid services. The protocol capabilities for file transfers as well as streaming have been presented in conjunction with the buffers used for PIPT communication and the threads for realizing the different communication patterns. To use Flex-SwA with web services, an integration with Apache Axis has been presented. For Grid services, Flex-SwA has been integrated into the Globus Toolkit.

The implementation of the Web and Grid Service Browser as a Firefox Add-on has been presented in detail. Besides the three XPCOM components stream converter, observer, Java Bridge, a user interface generator, an execution engine, and a result presentation engine have been implemented in Java. The components can be executed remotely by a servlet or locally from the Add-on. For user interface generation and result presentation, a WSDL and XML Schema parser built with the help of the XML2Java model generator has been implemented. To alleviate the search of Grid services, a search engine has been presented.

The Service-enabled Mashup Editor has been implemented as a Rich Internet Application with Adobe Flex. Flex applications are compiled to .swf files that run in the widely spread Adobe Flash Player. The editor can easily be extended with new components. A developer and user view have been implemented using Flex' states and state transitions. Grid service invocations are achieved using a proxy implemented as a Java servlet.

9
Evaluation

9.1 Introduction

With the continuous growth of video data, there is an increasing demand for video content analysis and indexing to effectively support video databases and retrieval systems. Typical tasks for video content analysis such as cut, face, or text detection are computationally demanding and require distributed (high-performance) resources for parallel processing to guarantee an acceptable run-time behavior. Since media analysis deals with computationally intensive tasks, it is reasonable to divide the analysis into several steps, such that single analysis steps can be distributed to different nodes. The paradigm of a service-oriented architecture (SOA) promises that these computationally intensive tasks can be exposed as services and effectively combined to new applications, thus speeding up application development. For the combination of these services (called orchestration), it is reasonable to use WS-BPEL (or simply BPEL), the de facto standard for workflows in industry, allowing companies to integrate multimedia services into their existing service portfolio.

However, since all service data pass the BPEL engine, the application of BPEL to data-intensive applications from the multimedia domain is not very efficient. Furthermore, the development of web services is still difficult and time-consuming, and in practice almost impossible for most of the end users. To obtain a broader user basis, it is necessary to simplify the use of web services. Also, in order to provide a timely execution, a distributed infrastructure for multimedia processing should scale easily.

In this chapter, a service-oriented architecture for multimedia applications is presented to address these issues. The developed Flex-SwA framework enables the modeling of data flows in BPEL. This way, an efficient and flexible data transfer in BPEL workflows is possible for multimedia applications. The tools developed in this thesis are illustrated, namely: 1. the Web and Grid Service Browser and 2. the Service-enabled Mashup Editor to easily use services. Additionally the Visual Grid Orchestrator (developed by Dörnemann et al. [35]) is used to create new services from existing ones. Scalability is achieved by the possibility to dynamically allocate resources from a computational Cloud, such as the Amazon Elastic Compute Cloud [12]. Furthermore, it is shown how a communication policy, embedded in the service's WSDL document, can be used to describe the protocol requirements of services in order to support real-time, streaming, or file transfer requirements. Finally, it is shown how a temporal policy manages the handling of communication policies.

Three case studies covering a broad multimedia scope are presented to show the technologies and tools providing conceptual improvements as well as improvements in terms of usability, ease of development, and efficiency. An audio resynthesis service, a face detector service, and a video-on-demand service are analyzed in detail and shown along with experimental results. The video-on-demand service is modernized by gradually switching from an old Java Media Framework multicast implementation based on the Real-time Transport Protocol (RTP) to a modern one based on the widely used Real-Time Messaging Protocol (RTMP) from Adobe realized with the Wowza Media Server 1.6. This change is described by means of temporal and communication policies. *Parts of this chapter have been published in [87, 52].*

9.2 A Service-Oriented Architecture for Multimedia Processing

At first glance, the SOA paradigm seems to be an appropriate solution for multimedia tasks. But in order to build a *Multimedia SOA* with a suitable set of tools and technologies, the general roles of a SOA, the structure of typical multimedia workflows as well as the implications of using BPEL, scalability issues, and topics like ease-of-use have to be taken into account.

9.2.1 General Roles in a Multimedia SOA

In a typical SOA, many roles can be distinguished [61]. However, for a SOA for multimedia analysis, a coarse distinction between different roles is sufficient. Figure 9.1 shows a model of the general actors involved in a Multimedia SOA along with some of their requirements.

A **service developer** is interested in an easy way to develop new applications and services. (S)he is assisted in this task by using additional middleware technologies for the transfer of large amounts of data that cannot be managed efficiently via SOAP. Using a workflow editor, a service developer combines low-

9.2. A Service-Oriented Architecture for Multimedia Processing

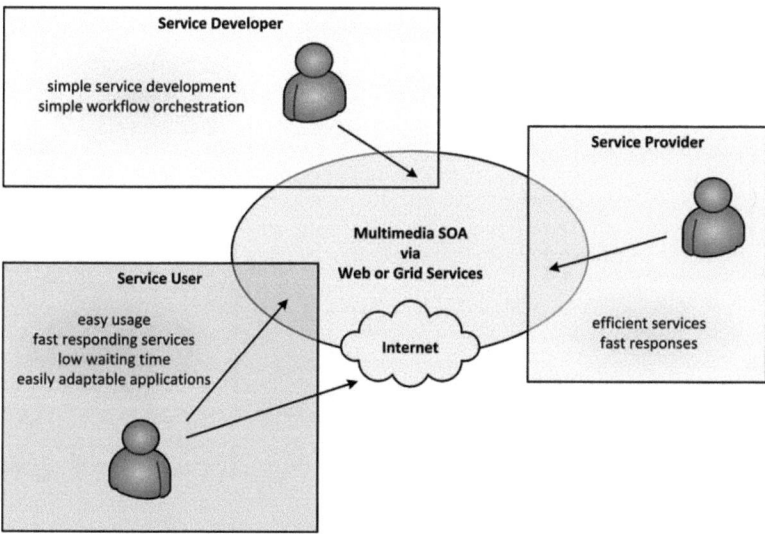

Figure 9.1: General roles in a multimedia SOA.

level services such as feature extraction and classification to new high-level services such as face detection or cut detection in videos, speaker recognition in audio streams, and so on.

The **service provider** is interested in efficient services, in the sense that the response time is minimized for the users. File transfers should be handled efficiently, thus reducing the response time of the service for the user.

The **service user** is interested in using services in an easy manner. For this reason, a browser able to handle WSDL descriptions of web services is useful. Some of the users might be interested in modifying their applications or creating new ones. This can be achieved by a mashup editor. A mashup editor should be offered as an Rich Internet Application (RIA) based on widely spread technologies like Flash, JavaScript, or other highly compatible technologies to avoid forcing users to perform difficult installations.

9.2.2 Structure of a Multimedia Workflow

Most approaches for content analysis are built in a monolithic fashion following a sequential structure (see Figure 9.2 and Eide et al. [36]) and are divided into two phases: training and classification. In general, preparatory tasks are executed to generate the smallest entities of interest needed to solve the problem in question, e.g., retrieving images from a database, decoding frames of a video, or decompressing audio signals. Next, some preprocessing is done, such as transforming or filtering. Then, the basic step of feature extraction is performed, followed by the actual classification. Sometimes, a postprocessing step is needed, e.g., building a representation of the analysis results. The training phase is similar, but a training step instead of a classification step is performed.

The classification step can be seen as a feature extraction step offering the opportunity to combine it with other features for building more complex analysis approaches.

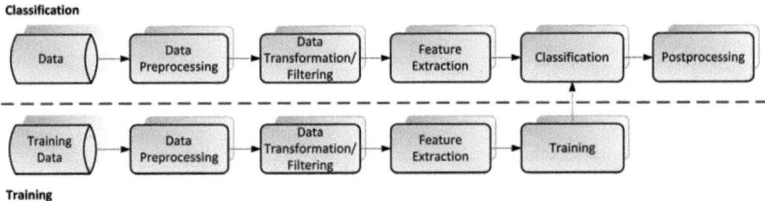

Figure 9.2: Multimedia analysis procedure.

The different tasks in the sequential structure are candidates to be extracted and wrapped as services. By allowing the composition or reconfiguration of ex-

9.2. A Service-Oriented Architecture for Multimedia Processing

isting services, workflow languages speed up the development of distributed multimedia analysis applications.

9.2.3 Modeling the Data Flow in BPEL4WS

BPEL as an orchestration language for business processes defines a workflow as a set of activities. These activities are divided into two groups: basic and structured. The basic activities describe single steps for the interaction with a service and/or the manipulation of data passing the engine. With structured activities, the order of activity execution is dictated. Thus, BPEL provides a rich set of elements to explicitly model the control flow (i.e. sequence of invocations, fault handling, etc.), but the data flow is only modeled implicitly by the manipulation and assignment of data encapsulated in request/response messages. For example, the normal way of modeling the data exchange between two simple web services is as follows: invoke the first service with a request message, wait for the corresponding response from the service, assign all needed data to the input variable of the second service, invoke it with a request message encapsulating the data and finally wait for the response. In the context of highly frequent data exchange and transfer of large amounts of data, this way of modeling the data flow is not efficient.

Figure 9.3a shows the typical sequence of service invocations and the corresponding data flow. For example, the workflow engine invokes a preprocessing service and sends the multimedia data (A) to it. The service returns results (B) to the workflow engine, and these results are again transferred to one or more other services which perform the next step of multimedia analysis. Clearly, some of the data ((B) and (C)) is at least transferred twice. If, for example, Service 1 is a video splitter service, the video would be transferred to the video splitter and the video parts back to the BPEL engine and then to different services. This induces a significant load on the BPEL engine.

To reduce the load on the BPEL engine, references can be used to achieve efficient data transmissions in BPEL workflows. Figure 9.3b shows the data flow via *references* under full control of the BPEL engine. A reference points to a resource location in memory or to a file. The service can pull the data from the resource location directly. The data does not have to be sent to the BPEL engine, only the references have to be sent. Since the references are very small, the load on the BPEL engine is very small, too. Thus, the use of *references* circumvents transferring data twice.

For services to which data is sent repetitively (for example, video frames are sent repetitively), two ways for modeling the data flow are proposed:

(1) For each resulting processing unit (video part, frame, audio sample, ...), a reference passes the BPEL engine and is sent to the destination service. This way, the BPEL engine keeps full control over the data flow. Furthermore, the control flow resides at the engine. Thus, it is possible to model conditional elements in

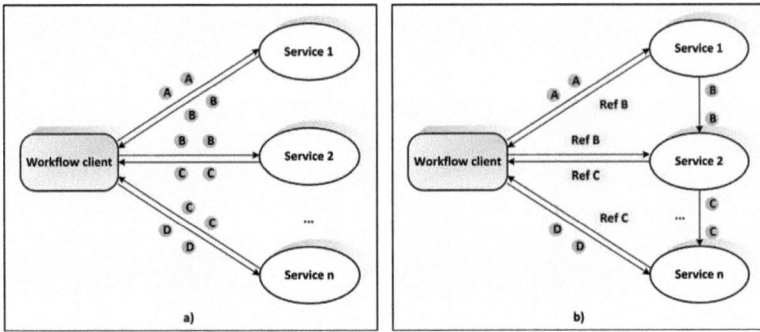

Figure 9.3: Data flow via a BPEL4WS engine.

reaction to the responses sent by the services. Failure and compensation handling is also possible in the workflow.

(2) For the communication to each service, a reference to a memory location is generated and the data is "streamed" from there. This way, it is possible to write to a memory location that the target service can read from. The BPEL engine is able to select the services that should communicate via the references, i.e. BPEL builds the streaming chain and eventually waits for a callback or control messages. Since even less data is transferred, this approach is expected to be very efficient.

9.2.4 Scalability

When using workflows, the endpoint of each service invocation is typically set statically [15]. However, if the demand for an actual workflow increases [37], the service invocations on a particular machine increase as well. With this increased demand, it is possible for these systems to become overloaded, resulting in the service's unavailability. If no explicit fault handling is performed within the workflow, the workflow will abort and computation time has been wasted.

To keep services available, an easy way is to extend the (hardware) platform on which the services are executed. In this way, the variety of resources for a certain service is larger and the load can be reduced in order to keep the services available. This is done manually by starting machines, deploying necessary software and, if necessary, adapting the workflow. Preferably, this should be done automatically.

A workflow engine should be used to track the load of the platform and, on system overload, dynamically provide new machines and perform service invocations on these new machines. Since it is possible that not a sufficient number of machines is available in-house for this dynamical growth, the use of so-called

9.2. A Service-Oriented Architecture for Multimedia Processing 125

Cloud resources is reasonable. The Amazon Elastic Compute Cloud (EC2) [12] is one example of such Cloud resources. The EC2 can dynamically provide new resources to be used for the platform in order to keep the system load at an acceptable level of quality. It offers a set of virtual machines for each user to deploy his or her applications.

Because startup (and shutdown, if the load decreases) of virtual machines are not performed by the EC2 itself, but by an external client, the workflow engine should handle these tasks.

9.2.5 Ease of Use

When offering web services in a SOA, there is often the problem that such services cannot be used easily. Client programs or portlets have to be written by the developers and a portal has to be offered by the service provider. Most WSDL files miss a working and easy to use client for invoking the web services. Potential web service users have to write their own client software to test and use a web service. Even if clients are available, they are often built for specific platforms, such as the Microsoft .NET framework. This limits their use to people using the Microsoft Windows operating system or to computer experts who know how to compile or build their own client software. Therefore, familiar web-based environments that can be installed easily, like a web browser or web sites with server-side software based on wide-spread technologies like HTML, JavaScript, Java, and Flash are desirable.

9.2.6 Multimedia SOA Layer Model

Taking the requirements of the different actors into account, the restrictions imposed by modeling the data flow with BPEL, the structure of typical multimedia workflows, and scalability and ease-of-use requirements, a layer model for a Multimedia SOA as shown in Figure 9.4 is proposed consisting of five layers: interaction layer, services and workflow layer, middleware layer, transport layer, and platform layer.

The *interaction layer* provides a frontend to communicate with the Multimedia SOA. A developer uses a BPEL workflow editor like the Grid-enabled Visual Grid Orchestrator (ViGO) to define new workflows out of existing services and workflows from the services and workflow layer. Workflows and single services can be executed by the Web and Grid Service Browser handling user interface generation and service execution. Service users may even create new applications by using a Service-enabled Mashup Editor that allows the combination of a predefined set of services (e.g., face detection) and web applications like Flickr, and so on.

The *services and workflow layer* consists of workflows and of services arranged in an arbitrary number of sublayers. Workflows consist of services and, possibly, other workflows. The services sublayers range from low-level services such as feature extraction, feature classification over higher level services such as face detection, cut detection to high level services like actor detection (answering questions such as "How many minutes was actor A on the screen?"). Services can be combined to new services across all sublayers. A communication policy describes the protocols on which a service relies when data transfers or streaming capabilities are needed. The temporal policies are used to manage the communication policies.

The *middleware layer* uses Flex-SwA to provide references to resources. These references are mainly used for streaming capabilities such as the repetitive sending of frame data or when large files, e.g., videos, have to be transferred, as SOAP is not well suited for both of these tasks. With the help of Flex-SwA the proposed data flow modeling approaches are integrated into the multimedia SOA.

The *transport layer* realizes the actual transmission of data from the interaction layer to services, between services on specific platforms, and from services to the interaction layer.

The *platform layer* provides the resources needed to execute the services. This includes dedicated as well as dynamic resources. The former ones are in-house desktop pools or cluster nodes. Dynamic resources can be virtual machines provided by EC2. A scalable infrastructure can be achieved using a dynamic provisioning component within the workflow engine as proposed by Dörnemann et al. [34].

9.3 Services of the Multimedia SOA

The goal of the multimedia SOA is to offer several analysis services and tools to easily use and recombine these services. Currently, the service offer comprises audio analysis services, video analysis services, and consumer services.

- **Audio Analysis Services**

    - **Automatic speaker diarization:** The service provides state-of-the-art techniques to perform speaker diarization: for a given input audio or video file, an index is created fully automatically that tells "who spoke when". This means finding all segments of speech and assigning those segments spoken by the same speaker to the same cluster.

    - **Feature extraction:** This service provides access to 21 different feature extraction methods, including well-known mel-frequency cepstral coefficients. Taking an audio or video file as input, the feature vectors according to the chosen method and parameter settings are returned.

    - **Voice model building:** Acoustic models (dedicated, but not limited to speech) can be build with this service. The user can choose among

9.3. Services of the Multimedia SOA

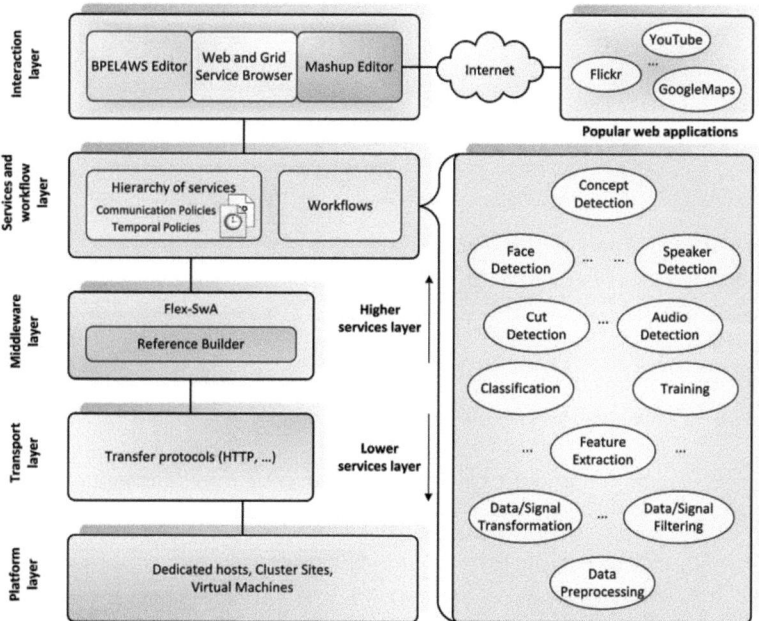

Figure 9.4: Layer model for a multimedia SOA.

all prevailing model types, including Gaussian mixture models, hidden Markov models, or one-class support vector machines.

– **Audio resynthesis:** The single steps of an audio analysis process bear many sources of confusion for potential users: the different methods of feature extraction or model building are complex in themselves, and a great number of available parameters for each method makes it difficult—even for an expert—to tell what effect a certain choice may have on the final result. The service offers methods to resynthesize the results of a specific analysis step using a specific parameter setting. A user then can listen to the result and thus gain intuitive insight into the effects of his selections from the way it sounds. The term resynthesis means the synthesis of a sound from features or models (that have previously been built from an audio file, thus "re"-synthesis) in a way that strives not for a pleasing or natural sound but for an audible representation that makes the settings of the feature/model perceivable.

- **Video Analysis Services**

    – **Decoder**: The decoder service decompresses MPEG-1 and MPEG-2 video files and outputs single video frames.

    – **Feature Extractor:** This service computes the dissimilarity of consecutive video frames by means of color histogram differences and motion compensated pixel differences. These features are used by the shot boundary detector.

    – **Shot Boundary Detector:** The temporal segmentation into meaningful units is an essential prerequisite for video indexing and retrieval purposes. Shots are separated in a video by abrupt shot changes (cuts) and gradual shot transitions such as fade and dissolve.

    – **MP7 Converter:** MPEG-7 [84] is an ISO standard that formalizes the description of metadata for multimedia documents. Basically, the MP7 service transforms analysis results (e.g., the result of temporal video segmentation) into a description that is compliant to the MPEG-7 standard and outputs corresponding MP7-files. Furthermore, the service is capable of merging several MPEG-7 input files into a single MPEG-7 representation.

    – **Video Face Detector**: The Video Face Detector service detects frontal faces in a video frame. This service is based on Intel's Open Source Computer Vision Library OpenCV [59] implementation of the face detector that has been originally proposed by Viola and Jones [97].

9.3. Services of the Multimedia SOA 129

- **Video Splitter**: The video splitter splits MPEG-1 and MPEG-2 video files into MPEG-1 and MPEG-2 video parts.

- **Consumer Services**

    - **Video on demand:** A user may invoke the video-on-demand service to either subscribe to a video-on-demand multicast based on the RTP or the RTMP protocol.

9.3.1 Use Cases

For evaluation purposes, three use cases have been selected—one from each domain.

Audio Resynthesis.

For the audio analysis, the audio resynthesis service called `WebVoice` is evaluated. It offers four different operations that make the intermediate result at specific points in the analysis process audible.

- **wav2splice:** This operation produces a "spliced" version of the input audio: the original signal is segmented into blocks of specifiable length; the time order of these blocks is then randomized. This helps analyzing the effect of time ordering on the perception of an audio signal.

- **wav2features:** Here, mel frequency cepstral coefficients (MFCCs) are extracted from the given audio signal based on the given parameter setting. The feature vectors are then resynthesized to a signal, helping the user to understand the effects of different parameter settings like pre-emphasis, filter bank size, or number of coefficients.

- **wav2gmm:** This is one of two operations to build a statistical model from audio features (that are automatically extracted from the given audio signal). It allows to configure the creation of a Gaussian mixture model with full or diagonal covariance matrix. The result is a signal resynthesized from feature vectors (MFCCs) that are drawn from the model according to the probability density function it represents. Listening to it evokes a sense of what the model represents in general.

- **wav2hmm:** This operation uses a hidden Markov model for resynthesis as stated above.

The evaluation of this use case will show that Flex-SwA is a more efficient and flexible technology for transferring bulk data (in this case, a wave file) than standard mechanisms like SOAP Messages with Attachments (SwA) and SOAP itself. The different communication patterns allow to investigate the best configuration for the data transfers that may also rely on the underlying hardware (e.g., multicore or single-core processors). Furthermore, for the interaction with the service, the functionality of the Web and Grid Service Browser as a tool dealing with web or Grid services in general and multimedia services especially is shown.

Video Face Detection.

From the domain of video analysis, a simple workflow consisting of three services for the task of face detection in videos is presented. Three variations of this workflow are discussed, each of them using a different style of data transmission.

A monolithic implementation for face detection typically consists of the following steps:

1. An MPEG decoder sequentially produces a series of frames from a given input video.

2. Each decoded frame is processed by a face detection algorithm mainly consisting of feature extraction and classification. The results of this algorithm are bounding rectangles stored in a simple list.

3. After processing the whole input video in this manner, a final list is given to a component using this information to build an MPEG-7 result file containing metainformation for the multimedia data.

This monolithic implementation can be decomposed by wrapping the functionality performed in the single steps into services. A service-oriented realization could, for example, cover three services: MPEG decoder, face detector, and MPEG-7 converter. Three different workflows have been designed using these services, each one with a different data transfer style.

- The first workflow relies strictly on the exchange of SOAP messages. Decoded frames and detected faces are encapsulated in these messages and delegated by the orchestration engine to the face detection service and MPEG-7 converter service.

- The second workflow uses Flex-SwA's reference concept; the data remains in the memory of the data producer (decoder or face detector) and only a small reference is transmitted in a SOAP message from the producer via the orchestration engine to the consumer (face detector or MPEG-7 converter) who can then pull the data directly.

- The last workflow uses Flex-SwA, too. Just one reference is delegated from the decoder over the engine to the face detector and another reference from the face detector over the engine to the MPEG-7 converter. These two

9.3. Services of the Multimedia SOA 131

references are used to install a fixed connection between the services for frame and face data transmission, such that a service can read the data directly from the producer repetitively.

The evaluation of this use case will show that the two proposed approaches to model the data flow explicitly using Flex-SwA in BPEL workflows are significantly more efficient than modeling the data flow implicitly. One approach leaves full control of the data flow at the BPEL engine, the other approach shifts control of the data flow to Flex-SwA. The design of the three workflows has been alleviated by the ViGO workflow editor. The interaction between user and services takes again place by using the Web and Grid Service Browser.

Video on Demand.

From the area of consumer services, an evaluation of a video-on-demand (VOD) service is presented. The integration of the VOD service will show the limits of web services with respect to streaming, soft real-time requirements and file transfers.

There are two main ways to organize the transmission of a video in a VOD application:

(1) The video is completely transferred to the end user before playback is started. Thus, the user can skip parts of the video.

(2) The video is streamed in "real-time" to the user or partially buffered. Thus, the user cannot jump forward to parts not yet received.

The first possibility is not very well suited if a user wants to watch a video ad-hoc, since transferring the video may take a lot of time. Using SOAP even makes the situation worse. The second possibility is the more suitable (and very popular, e.g., see youtube.com) one for watching videos in an ad-hoc manner. If the video is sent to several customers, RTP [86] will possibly be used for the transmission. Another possibility is to use TCP for a point-to-point communication and buffer parts of the video locally before starting to watch the video. To integrate the VOD application into a SOA with standardized web service technologies, the RTP packets have to be sent over SOAP.

The evaluation of this service shows that it is at least hard to achieve a SOAP-based VOD service with a sufficient performance. Three scenarios are presented, each showing a different degree of integration into the SOA. The first scenario presents a standard VOD application that is not integrated into the SOA. The second scenario presents a service that realizes the RTP communication over SOAP. The third scenario shows how a communication policy can be utilized to express the need for RTP as the communication protocol and integrate it into the SOA.

The user interacts with the video-on-demand service by help of the Service-enabled Mashup Editor that supports the RTMP protocol.

9.3.2 Implementation Issues

The implementation of the described services has either been realized as web or Grid services. Web services are basically stateless meaning that between two invocations, a web service does not remember information about its clients. Grid services, on the other hand, manage states according to the Web Service Resource Framework (WSRF) [46] and can thus provide information about their current progress usable for long service runs.

The `WebVoice` service for audio resynthesis is based on the `sclib` library. This C++ class library is currently under development at the University of Marburg, Germany, and provides state-of-the-art speaker recognition and related algorithms, methods and tools under a unified interface. The service has been implemented as a web service in Apache Axis 1.4 since it "only" takes a plain wave (16kHz, 16bit mono channel MS-RIFF WAV format) file as input and returns another wave file representing the selected features. Up to now, the service works in a monolithic fashion, such that a parallelization is not yet possible. But since the implementation of the service is efficient, it might be sufficient to replicate the service.

The video face detection service has been realized by implementing several Grid services in Java with the help of the "Service Generator" of the Grid Development Tools (GDT) [42]. As a Grid middleware, the widespread Globus Toolkit (4.0.7) [39] was used. Since the feature extraction task of the face detection algorithm is the most time consuming task, it is desirable to parallelize that task. The use of Grid services allows to move these services to a virtualized cluster in the future.

The first Grid service wraps an MPEG-Decoder written in C++, the second one is the video face detector that uses the algorithms of the OpenCV library [59], and the third one converts the analysis results of the preceding service into a standard MPEG-7 file. All services publish several methods to support the different workflows.

The additional features that Grid services offer also require a more complex implementation. Since the use of Grid services is not directly supported by graphical workflow modeling tools in the BPEL environment, the BPEL-based workflows have been designed with the Visual Grid Orchestrator (ViGO), a BPEL editor able to design workflows consisting of Grid services and a modified ActiveBPEL engine [35] able to handle Grid service invocations and platform integration (e.g., Amazon EC2).

The VOD service has been implemented with the help of the Java Media Framework. The Java Media Framework provides an RTP implementation that can be used to stream videos over the network. An YouTube frontend has been implemented as an Adobe Flex component.

9.4 Quantitative Evaluation of the Use Cases

After describing the use cases and their implementation, a quantitative evaluation of the use cases is presented.

9.4.1 Audio Resynthesis (WebVoice)

The WebVoice service was tested with the different Flex-SwA communication and memory patterns in order to determine the most efficient pattern for the underlying hardware and operating system (Pentium D 3 GHz (dual-core), with 3 GB of RAM and the Microsoft Windows XP Professional SP2 operating system). The client was executed on another computer with the same specifications on the same LAN. The implementation of the service may depend on the pattern used. If a lazy pattern is used, the implementation effort may increase. Listing 9.1 shows the implementation of the wav2splice operation of the WebVoice service used for all communication and memory patterns except for lazy nonblocking.

```
public Reference[] wav2splice(Reference[] ref,
  boolean usePhaseSynthesis, int preservedBlockSize,
  int intermediateFrameCount, double steepness,
  double olaErrorTarget, int olaMaxIterationCount)
{
  Reference[] res = new Reference[ref.length];
  for (int i = 0; i < ref.length; i++)
  {
    InputStream is = ref[i].acquire();
    SC_Wrapper wrapper = new SC_Wrapper();
    String fName = wrapper.wav2splice(is,
      "fb12_webvoice/webvoice.ini",
      FlexSwAConstants.getFileServerDir(),
      usePhaseSynthesis, preservedBlockSize,
      intermediateFrameCount, steepness,
      olaErrorTarget, olaMaxIterationCount);
    res[i] = returnReferenceFromString(fName);
    is.close();
    return res;
  }
}
```

Listing 9.1: Implementation of the wav2splice operation (exception handling omitted).

The `wav2splice` operation of the `WebVoice` service takes an array of references and the parameters for the actual C++ `wav2splice` function. The command `ref[i].acquire()` loads the referenced data either from the local disk or memory or from the remote machine to the local disk or memory depending on the communication or memory pattern specified. For the lazy nonblocking variant of the service, the implementation is shown in Listing 9.2.

```
public Reference[] wav2splice(Reference[] ref,
    boolean usePhaseSynthesis, int preservedBlockSize,
    int intermediateFrameCount, double steepness,
    double olaErrorTarget, int olaMaxIterationCount)
{
  Reference[] res = new Reference[ref.length];
  InputStream[] is = new InputStream[ref.length];
  for (int i = 0; i < ref.length; i++)
  {
    is[i] = ref[i].acquire();
  }
  for (int i = 0; i < ref.length; i++)
  {
    SemaphoreRegistry.getInstance()
      .acquire(ref[i].getUrid());
    SC_Wrapper wrapper = new SC_Wrapper();
    String fName = wrapper.wav2splice(is[i],
      "fb12_webvoice/webvoice.ini",
      FlexSwAConstants.getFileServerDir(),
      usePhaseSynthesis, preservedBlockSize,
      intermediateFrameCount, steepness,
      olaErrorTarget, olaMaxIterationCount);
    res[i] = returnReferenceFromString(fName);
    is[i].close();
    return res;
  }
}
```

Listing 9.2: Implementation of the lazy nonblocking variant of the `wav2splice` operation (exception handling omitted).

The loading of the referenced data is initiated for all files before the analysis of the first wave file starts. Since the nonblocking pattern is used for the service, the `ref[i].acquire()` command does not block. Before a wave file is given to the sclib, asking the `SemaphoreRegistry` ensures that the data referenced by the `Reference` object has been completely transferred, which is a requirement for the sclib.

9.4. Quantitative Evaluation of the Use Cases 135

As a reference implementation, an SwA implementation of the `wav2splice` operation was used, as shown in Listing 9.3.

```
public Reference[] wav2splice(boolean usePhaseSynthesis,
  int preservedBlockSize, int intermediateFrameCount,
  double steepness, double olaErrorTarget,
  int olaMaxIterationCount)
{
  int i = 0;
  Message m =
    MessageContext.getCurrentContext().getCurrentMessage();
  Reference[] res = new Reference[m.countAttachments()];
  Iterator<AttachmentPart> it = m.getAttachments();
  while (it.hasNext())
  {
    AttachmentPart a = it.next();
    InputStream in = (InputStream) a.getContent();
    SC_Wrapper wrapper = new SC_Wrapper();
    String fName = wrapper.wav2splice(in,
    "fb12_webvoice/webvoice.ini",
    FlexSwAConstants.getFileServerDir(), usePhaseSynthesis,
    preservedBlockSize, intermediateFrameCount, steepness,
    olaErrorTarget, olaMaxIterationCount);
    res[i] = returnReferenceFromString(fName);
    i++;
  }
  in.close();
  return res;
}
```

Listing 9.3: Implementation of the `wav2splice` operation with SwA (exception handling omitted).

In the SwA implementation, the attachments have to be detached of the SOAP message (if needed) by iterating over the attachment parts of the SOAP message. From each attachment part, the input stream is given to the `wav2splice` C++ function.

The average processing time of the service was measured for 50 runs from the client's machine. The measurements consist of transferring five wave files, each sized 9.5 MB, to the service, analyzing the files and returning a reference to the spliced files. The red bar (Analysis) in Figure 9.5 indicates the time needed for the analysis of these five audio files. The other bars show the time of the data transfers (i.e. analysis *and* data transfers) for the different communication patterns and for SwA.

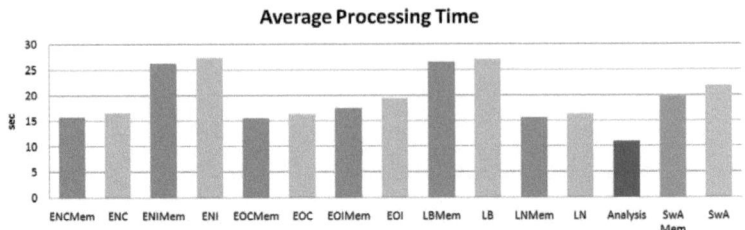

Figure 9.5: Average processing time of the wav2splice operation.

The analysis of the five audio files took 10.87sec on the average. When using SwA for the data transfer, the time for analysis and data transfers was 19.82sec when directly handling the content of the SOAP message (SwA Mem) or 21.88sec when the received attachments had first been written to the local disk and then processed by the sclib (SwA). When using one of the concurrent memory modes, the processing time speeds up to 15.62sec (ENC mem), 15.51sec (EOC mem), and 15.60sec (LN mem). The concurrent persistent modes are a little slower: 16.51sec (ENC), 16.33sec (EOC), and 16.31sec (LN). The modes where the data transfer is done iteratively before the analysis are slower compared to SwA because five different connections are used to transfer the data: 26.25sec (ENI mem), 26.55sec (LB mem), 27.35sec (ENI), 27.06sec (LB). Although the EOI mem and EOI modes are iterative modes, they perform a little faster than SwA and SwA mem due to overlapping of the service execution and data transmission. After the first file has arrived, the analysis and the data transfers are executed concurrently. Generally, when handling the data in memory, the processing is a little faster.

Figure 9.6 shows the standard deviation; it is below 0.7sec for all experiments.

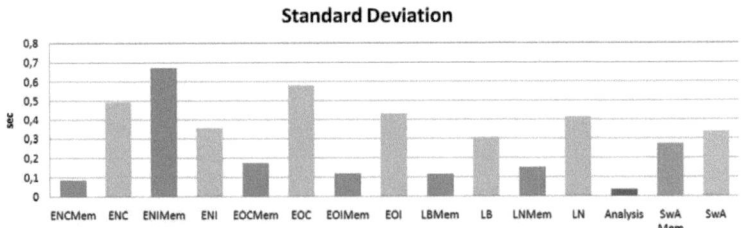

Figure 9.6: Standard deviation for invoking the wav2splice operation.

Using Flex-SwA has the further advantage that the memory footprint at the

9.4. Quantitative Evaluation of the Use Cases

client side is smaller. The client-side memory usage for the different patterns and SwA is shown in Figure 9.7. While the `WebVoice` Flex-SwA client does not need more than $4.41MB$ of heap size for the different patterns, the `WebVoice` SwA client already needs $268.67MB$. The problem is even more severe for larger files. This problem is due to the implementation of SwA in Apache Axis. But the problem that an attachment is loaded to memory as a whole on the client or server side persists.

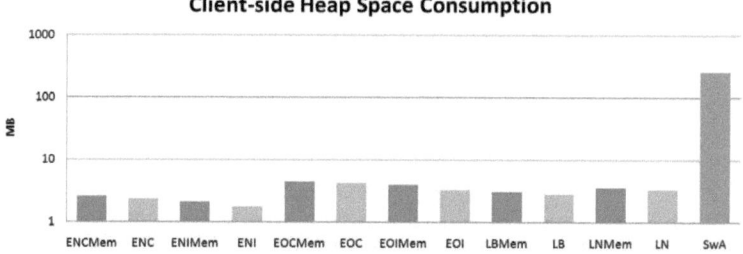

Figure 9.7: Client-side heap space consumption.

To summarize, the evaluation of the Flex-SwA communication and memory patterns exemplified by an audio resynthesis service has shown that selecting the correct communication patterns can speed up the processing time of the service by either overlapping data transfers and service execution or handling data transfers concurrently. In addition, the use of Flex-SwA reduces the development effort compared with SwA.

9.4.2 Face Detection in Videos

For the face detection service, four different scenarios are investigated and compared with the performance of the monolithic implementation to determine the overhead of using ActiveBPEL, Globus Toolkit, and of distributing this scenario within a local area network.

In the first scenario, the *original* implementation of the video analysis running on a Pentium D 3 GHz (dual-core) with 3 GB of RAM and the Microsoft Windows XP Professional SP2 operating system is tested. In the second scenario, the different video analysis services are deployed to the Globus service container and executed by the ActiveBPEL engine. The ActiveBPEL engine and the Globus service container are running on the same computer. For the third scenario, four computers are used. The ActiveBPEL engine is running on a Core 2 Duo with 3 GHz and 2 GB RAM and the Fedora 9 operating system. The Globus middleware is distributed to three computers each with a Pentium D 3 GHz (dual-core), with 3

GB of RAM, and the Microsoft Windows XP Professional SP2 operating system. The computers are connected by a 100 Mbit/s Fast Ethernet network.

For the second and third scenario, the total time of the analysis is measured 1.) when decoded frames and detected faces are sent in SOAP messages, 2.) when a Flex-SwA reference is sent for *each* decoded frame and detected face, and 3.) when the data is streamed directly without passing the ActiveBPEL engine at all. Normally, SOAP messages with Attachments (SwA) would be used for binary data instead of normal SOAP, but SwA is not supported by Globus Toolkit 4.0.x. Because sending of uncompressed frame information as an array in SOAP messages leads to large messages of approximately 5 MB, all array structures were transformed to simple strings leading to a size of approximately 1 MB.

A fourth scenario tests how much time the face detection service needs on the Amazon EC2. Normal SOAP messages are sent in this scenario.

In the first three scenarios, two videos from the TRECVID 2006 test set were analyzed. In the last scenario, only the second TRECVID video was tested. Each analysis was run 20 times. The results of the first three analysis (consisting of the average of the measured total times) are shown in Figures 9.8 and 9.9. In all scenarios, the video has been transferred to the first service before the service is invoked and the measurement begins.

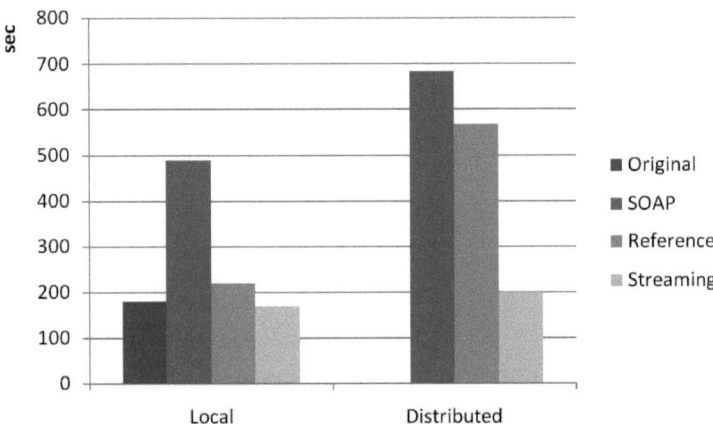

Figure 9.8: Analysis runtimes for 20051227_125800_CNN_LIVEFROM_ENG.

The total time of the original implementation is used as a reference for the other scenarios. Figure 9.8 shows the results for the first video, Figure 9.9 shows the results for the second video. In the diagrams, time measurements for four dif-

9.4. Quantitative Evaluation of the Use Cases

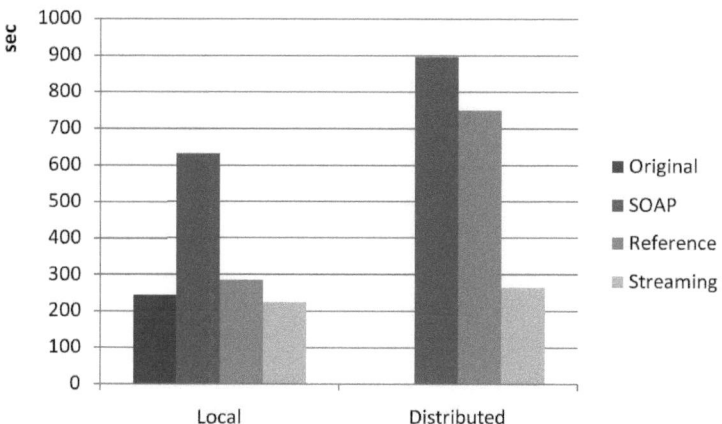

Figure 9.9: Analysis runtimes for 20051209_125800_CNN_LIVEFROM_ENG.

ferent local implementations are presented. The first local implementation is the original monolithic implementation; analyzing the first video took approximately 180 seconds, analyzing the second video took 244 seconds (188/244). Analyzing the same videos using SOAP took approximately 490/631 seconds. When using references, the analysis speeded up (219/286 seconds) compared to the SOAP version. Using the streaming capabilities is even slightly faster than the original implementation: The analysis took approximately 170/225 seconds. While the original monolithic implementation is not multithreaded, the services are capable of using several threads leveraging the parallel processing provided by the dual core, thus resulting in a faster execution of the analysis.

In the tests with a distributed environment, each service is placed on a different computer. The data transmission via SOAP messages took approximately 683/896 seconds. The references approach speeded up the total time of the distributed analysis to 570/749 seconds. The distributed streaming approach, however, is the fastest approach; it is nearly as fast as the local streaming approach and needs 200/264 seconds.

In the distributed environment, the reference approach is slower than the streaming approach, since a SOAP message has to be sent and processed for each frame, whereas in the streaming approach only one SOAP message has to be sent and processed.

The two proposed approaches based on the extended Flex-SwA framework outperform normal SOAP messages. The streaming approach is much faster than the other approaches at the price of breaking the normal orchestration approach. The communication is shifted to the services or Flex-SwA framework, respectively, bypassing the BPEL engine. The workflow engine, however, can—with additional implementation effort—control the data flow via callbacks.

For applications that do not necessarily need the best possible run-time behavior, the proposed reference approach is a suitable compromise between a good run-time behavior and leaving full control at the workflow engine. Furthermore, it is possible to send several frames via one reference resulting in a trade-off between data flow control and efficiency. This way, a developer may gradually shift from full data flow control to more efficiency.

To get a comparison between the execution on physical hosts and virtual machines, the analysis was also performed in a virtualized environment. Amazon EC2 was used. The start of a virtual machine within the EC2 needs a special image, a so-called Amazon Machine Image (AMI), which has to be prepared beforehand. Such an image contains the operating system and all necessary user libraries and code. In the presented case, an Ubuntu based Linux was used and the necessary native code as well as the middleware had to be deployed.

The ActiveBPEL workflow engine allows to use a special `invokehandler` to process invocations of services. The solution proposed by Dörnemann et al. [34] utilizes this mechanism to obtain a scalable infrastructure. For this aim, a service is assumed to be reachable via a prepared virtual machine. Listing 9.4 shows the corresponding partnerlink of the decoder when the dynamic scheduler is used. It can be seen that all necessary information for the EC2 (like *accessID* and *secretkey*) is passed to the `invokehandler`. When an invocation is performed on this particular partnerlink, the loadbalancer checks all hosts offering that special porttype for their load and performs the actual invoke on the host with the least load. If no such host is available, a new virtual machine within the EC2 is started and the invocation is carried out there.

```
<partnerLink name="decoderPL">
  <partnerRole endpointReference="dynamic"
    invokeHandler="java:LoadBalancer
    ?threshold=1.0;accessID=***;secretKey=***;
    imageID=ami-95cc28fc;availZone=us-east-1c"/>
```

Listing 9.4: Dynamic invokehandler within the BPEL process.

Amazon EC2 uses a "pay-as-you-go" model for pricing its resources. The storage, e.g., for the AMI, is priced by Amazon's S3 [13], so that each GB costs $0.15 per month. Computing power is priced per hour; the actual amount depends on the so-called Instance Type. Different Instance Types describe different machine setups. In the presented measurements only "small instances"[1] and "High-CPU

---

[1] 1.7 GB of memory, 1 EC2 Compute Unit (1 virtual core with 1 EC2 Compute Unit), 160

9.4. Quantitative Evaluation of the Use Cases

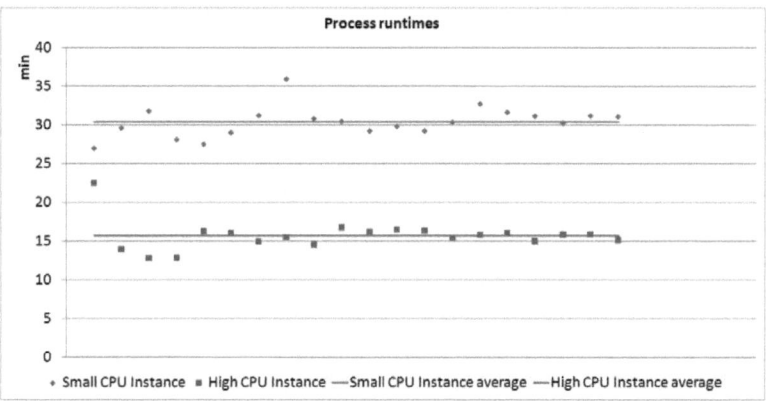

Figure 9.10: Process runtimes in a virtualized environment.

medium instances"[2] are used. The former one costs $0.10 and the latter one $0.20 per hour.

As before, a video from the TRECVID 2006 test (20051209_125800_CNN_LIVEFROM_ENG.mpg) was used, the messages were exchanged using pure SOAP. It can be seen in Figure 9.10 that when using the small instance type analyzing the video took around 1823.82 sec, whereas using the high-cpu instance type the analysis only took 941.29 sec. In comparison to Figure 9.9, the slow-down is around a factor of 2.04 for the small instance type and around a factor of 1.05 for the high-cpu instance type. Since the algorithms are single-threaded and the code is running in a virtual machine, this slow-down is acceptable. But the advantage of a dynamically scalable infrastructure redeems this small performance decrease.

9.4.3 Video-on-Demand

The video-on-demand service was evaluated in three different scenarios, as described in Section 9.3.1. In the first scenario, a video and audio stream is transmitted from and to localhost via RTP. The time for packaging and unpackaging the data has been measured on an Intel Centrino (1.5GHz clock speed, 2GB RAM) with the Windows XP SP2 operating system. The RTP packets were sent via UDP. At the sender, the time for packaging an RTP packet to a UDP data-

---

GB of instance storage, 32-bit platform. One EC2 Compute Unit (ECU) provides the equivalent CPU capacity of a 1.0-1.2 GHz 2007 Opteron or 2007 Xeon processor.

[2]1.7 GB of memory, 5 EC2 Compute Units (2 virtual cores with 2.5 EC2 Compute Units each), 350 GB of instance storage, 32-bit platform

gram and initiating the transmission has been measured. At the receiver, the multimedia stream was read and shown to the user. Here, the time for receiving the datagram and extracting the RTP packet from the datagram has been measured. The transmission of the video lasted 30 seconds and was repeated five times.

In the second scenario, the sender transmits each RTP packet over SOAP, i.e. every RTP packet is embedded into a SOAP message and then transmitted. Again, the time for packaging and unpackaging has been measured including the SOAP processing. The SOAP messages were sent via UDP. The Apache Axis serializer and deserializer were extracted from the Axis package, so that their capabilities could be used without using the SOAP engine as a whole. The sender serializes the RTP data with the Axis serializer as Base64Binary and then sends the SOAP message to the receiving endpoint as a UDP datagram. The receiver reads the datagram and then deserializes the RTP packet from the SOAP message. The time measured is expected to be higher since serialization and deserialization take place before transmission and after reception. Again, the transmission of the video lasted 30 seconds and was repeated five times.

Tables 9.1 and 9.2 summarize the results of these measurements. When the RTP communication is encapsulated over SOAP, the time for serialization induces an overhead of a factor of approximately 10 compared to the preparation time. The decapsulation process even introduces an overhead of a factor of 1000 and more. The standard deviation for one of the runs was especially high, namely approximately 113 ms. Since a video-on-demand application is a real-time application, outliers like this may not be neglected.

Table 9.1: Average time for preparing transmission and reception of a multimedia stream.

	average time for "packaging" in msec	average time for "unpackaging" in msec
RTP	0.1331-0.1360	0.0098-0.0137
RTP over SOAP	1.5710-1.6640	16.3163-18.9898

When comparing the quality of the video watching experience, it was noticeable that the video—when transmitted via SOAP messages—got stuck sometimes, even though it was not even transmitted over the network, such that network latencies can be excluded as a cause. Furthermore, the standard deviation of the receiving process shows that the time for deserialization varies more strongly than in the normal RTP case. Hence, when realizing the RTP communication over SOAP, the quality of the VOD service is not adequate for end users. One conclusion is that this type of application is not suitable for existing approaches

9.4. Quantitative Evaluation of the Use Cases 143

Table 9.2: Standard deviation for preparing transmission and reception of a multimedia stream.

	standard deviation for "packaging" in msec	standard deviation for "unpackaging" in msec
RTP	0.0436-0.0770	0.0072-0.0497
RTP over SOAP	11.1056-11.9470	27.0960-113.1239

based on web services. However, by applying the communication policy introduced in this thesis, it is possible to solve this problem without abstaining from web services, so that the advantages of web services like self-describing interfaces, loose coupling, etc. can be leveraged for this application.

This problem can be solved by relying on the protocols specifically designed for this type of application like RTP. When using a communication policy, as done in the third scenario, it is possible to declare the protocols an application depends on.

In the third scenario, it is shown how the VOD service can be integrated into a SOA using a communication policy. Instead of handling the RTP communication over SOAP, the communication policy describes the protocols suitable for such an application.

A simple video-on-demand web service starting a video transmission when invoked has been developed. It returns the endpoint of the multimedia stream to the client. The client uses the endpoint to receive the multimedia stream. An excerpt of the service's WSDL with an embedded communication policy is shown in Listing 9.5.

The policy shows that the service will use RTP and that the client has to support this protocol in order to invoke the service.

The time needed in the third scenario for the RTP communication (as shown in Table 9.3) is in the same dimension as the times of the first scenario, since only the pure packaging and unpackaging times have been measured. The service invocation itself is the only overhead compared to using the application without services. However, this could be anticipated, since the communication is still realized via RTP.

Thus, using the communication policy allows to even integrate services with soft real-time into the Multimedia SOA, which could otherwise hardly be integrated. The communication policy provides a standard way for these services to describe protocol needs with regard to file transfers, streaming, and real-time.

```
<?xml version="1.0" encoding="UTF-8"?>
<wsdl:definitions
 xmlns:cp="http://fb12.de/2007/05/communicationpolicy" ...>
 <wsp:Policy>
  <wsp:All>
   <wsp:ExactlyOne>
    <cp:protocol name="rtp" protocolID="RTPv2"
     operationref="streamVideo"/>
   </wsp:ExactlyOne>
  </wsp:All>
 </wsp:Policy>
 <wsdl:message name="streamVideoResponse">
  <wsdl:part name="streamVideoReturn" type="xsd:string"/>
 </wsdl:message>
 <wsdl:message name="streamVideoRequest">
  <wsdl:part name="videoname" type="xsd:string"/>
 </wsdl:message>
 <wsdl:portType name="VideoOnDemand">
  <wsdl:operation name="streamVideo">
   parameterOrder="videoname"
   <wsdl:input message="impl:streamVideoRequest"
    name="streamVideoRequest"/>
   <wsdl:output message="impl:streamVideoResponse"
    name="streamVideoResponse"/>
  </wsdl:operation>
 </wsdl:portType>
 ...
</wsdl:definitions>
```
Listing 9.5: Policy embedded in WSDL for a simple video-on-demand service.

Table 9.3: Average time for preparing transmission and reception of a multimedia stream.

	"packaging"	"unpackaging"
RTP with CP (average time in msec)	0.1339-0.1363	0.0096-0.0132
RTP with CP (standard deviation in msec)	0.0445-0.0753	0.0074-0.0504

9.5 Qualitative Evaluation of the Use Cases

Besides the quantitative evaluation, also a qualitative evaluation has been performed to evaluate the services from the user's perspective.

9.5.1 Audio Resynthesis (WebVoice)

In order to achieve a user-friendly but also generic interface for services, the Web and Grid Service Browser (realized as a Firefox plugin) is used. The Web and Grid Service Browser automatically generates a user interface when browsing to the WSDL of a service. It handles security configuration, proxy certificate generation when invoking Grid services and helps users to provide the relevant information to invoke the services and takes care of service invocation itself according to the style/use combinations. For multimedia data, the Web and Grid Service Browser provides special result presentations to make audio files audible and to visualize images and videos.

When a user normally browses to a WSDL description of a service, an XML tree appears as shown in Figure 9.11.

With the WSDL alone, a user without a computer science background will have severe problems invoking a service. The Web and Grid Service Browser, however, automatically generates a user interface when the user browses to the WSDL description of the service. The user interface that is generated when browsing to the WebVoice service's WSDL description is shown in Figure 9.12.

When the user slides over the operations drop down menu, a tooltip helps choosing the right operation. The form fields are already filled with the default values set in the XML schema part of the WSDL file. To transfer an audio file, the user pushes the browse button and selects a file from the hard disk. The audio file is then transferred to the web service via Flex-SwA. The data is pushed to the service if the user is in a private network. If the user has a public IP address, the local file is streamed to the service, such that the processing of the data can overlap with the transmission. After analysis, the result presentation engine generates an HTML page offering the user to download or listen to the resynthesized audio (see Figure 9.13).

In the first section of the result page, the data of the resulting SOAP message is shown. When the mouse slides over the white exclamation mark, the data type is shown as a tooltip. The second section is reserved for the original SOAP message (hidden in the screenshot). By clicking on the green "down" arrow, sections can be hidden and shown again. In the third section, a media player is embedded into the result page that plays the resynthesized audio file.

Therefore, normal computer users can simply invoke web services found on the web, especially web services processing and offering multimedia content.

146   Evaluation

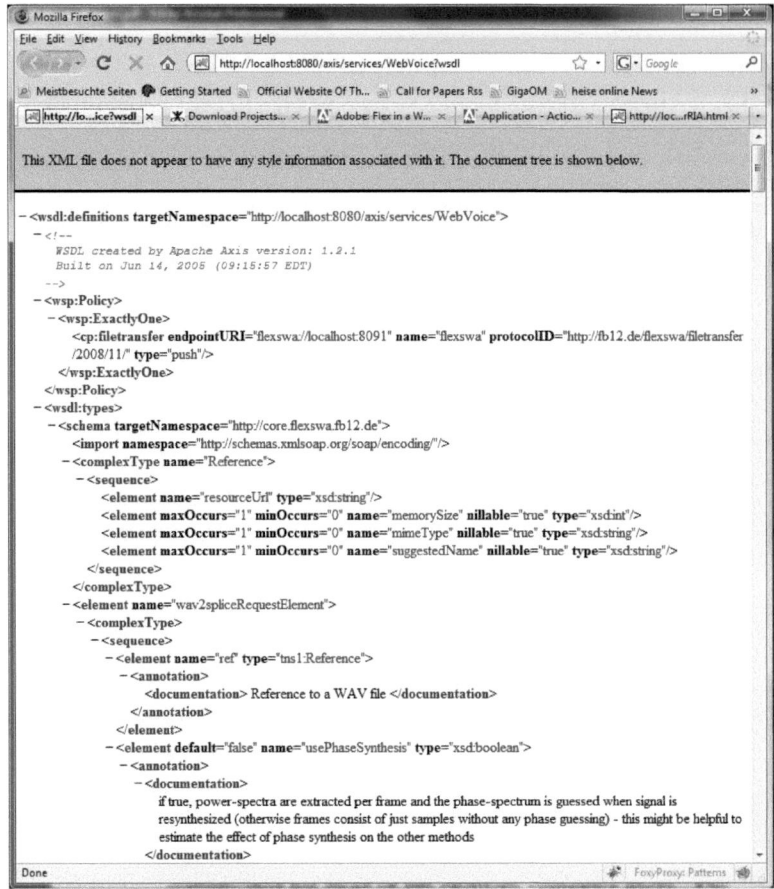

Figure 9.11: Screenshot of Firefox showing a WSDL file.

9.5. Qualitative Evaluation of the Use Cases

Figure 9.12: Screenshot of the `WebVoice` service user unterface.

9.5.2 Face Detection in Videos

The workflow built for face detection was already exposed as a web service for the quantitative evaluation. To enable a user to invoke the service easily, it is again reasonable to use the Web and Grid Service Browser. The user interface for invoking the service is similar to the user interface of the `WebVoice` service. The result presentation, however, looks different. An array of images is returned with the detected faces highlighted according to the MP7 file. The images are automatically visualized by the Web and Grid Services Browser as shown in Figure 9.14.

For the developer, the work is eased by using the Visual Grid Orchestrator (ViGO) to design the workflow as shown in Figure 9.15. When creating the workflow, the user is guided by wizards to add all necessary invokes. Afterwards, the user has to add all assign operations, model the data transfer and then—finally—create the links between the activities to express the control flow.

The use of ViGO in tandem with the Grid-enabled workflow engine leads to considerable simplifications in the development and the treatment of Grid workflows. Grid services can be handled like classic web services, making no difference in development and execution.

Because of the inherent startup of virtual machines, the use of the load balancer even allows to achieve a scalable infrastructure.

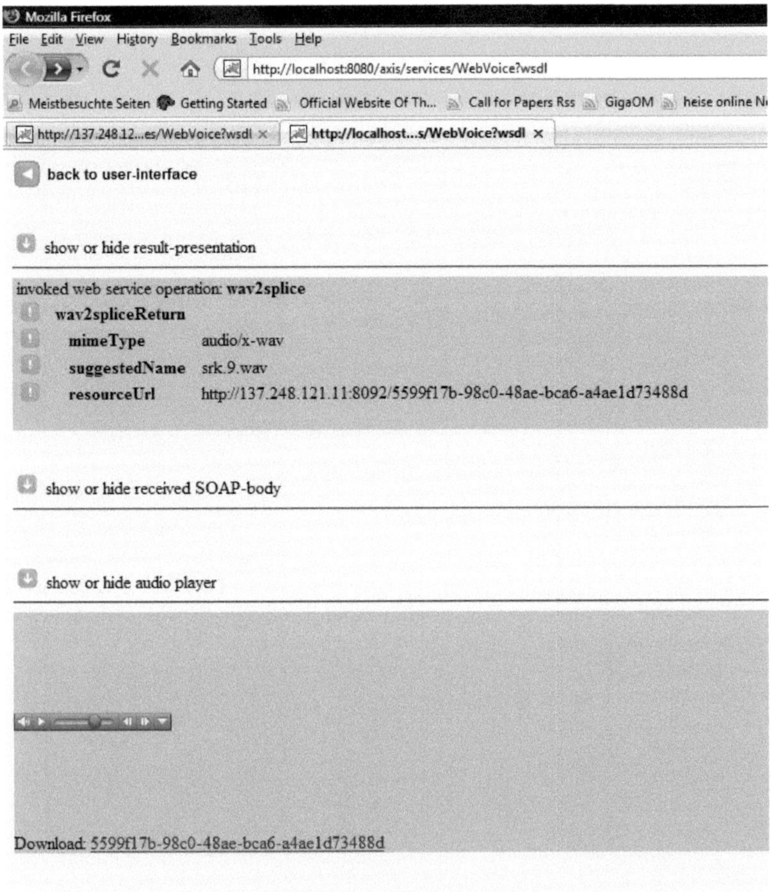

Figure 9.13: Result of the `wav2splice` operation.

9.5. Qualitative Evaluation of the Use Cases

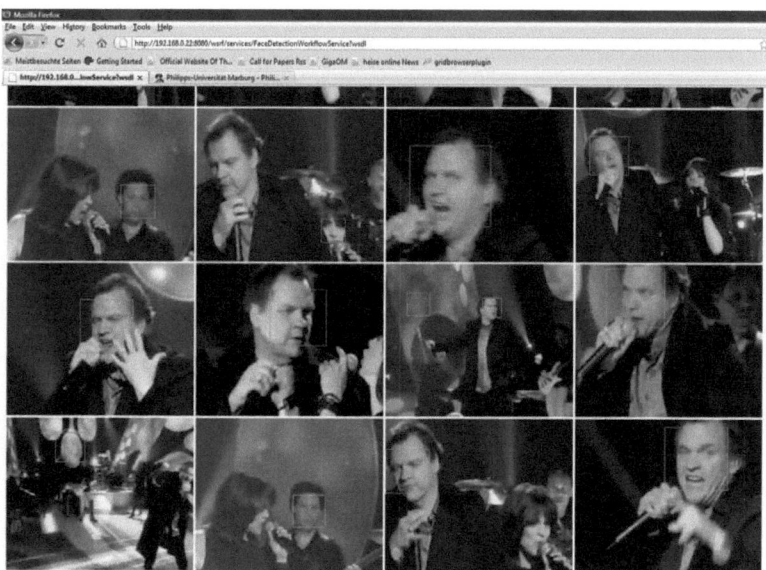

Figure 9.14: Screenshot of the results of the face detection workflow service for a Meat Loaf music video.

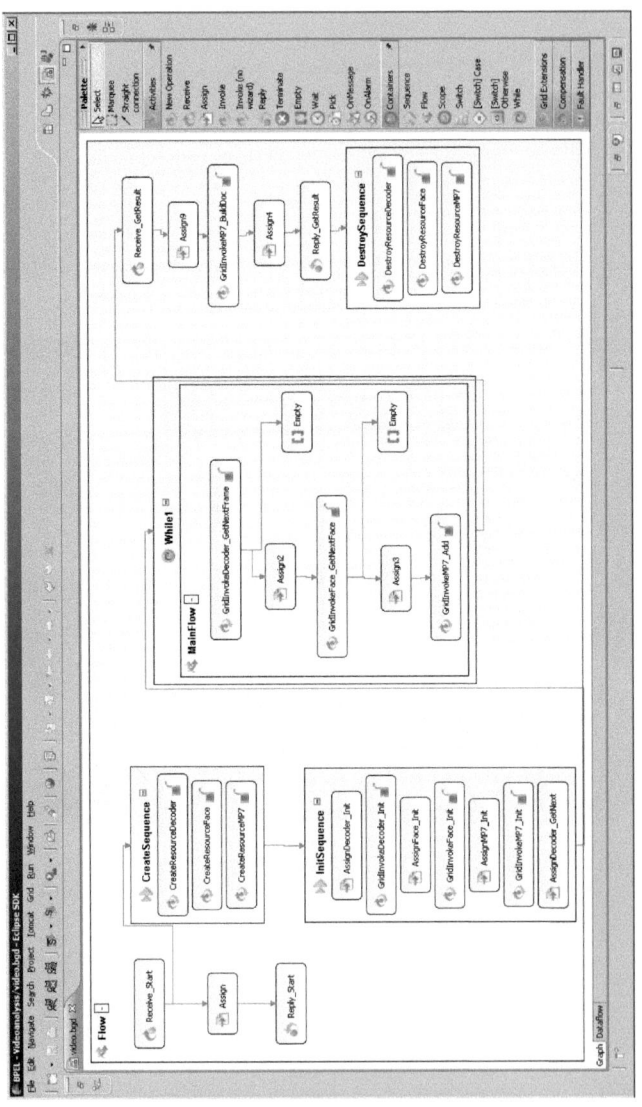

Figure 9.15: Screenshot of the face detection workflow in ViGO.

9.5.3 Video on Demand

The video-on-demand service was implemented with the Java Media Framework and is based on RTP. In the meantime, the FLV format as well as the proprietary RTMP protocol of Adobe (whose specification is to be released in the first half of 2009 [7]) has become popular and there are several players able to play video streams based on the format and protocol. Since there is a larger user group actually consuming these streams, it is a good idea to exchange the multicast implementation of the Java Media Framework with a multicast implementation based on RTMP and videos in the FLV format. For a gradual change of the video-on-demand service's protocol requirements, a temporal policy is used to describe the validity of changing communication policies. The policies are shown in Listing 9.6.

The temporal policy (shown in Listing 9.6a) expires on April 1st, 2009. Until that time, it uses the communication policy offering the multicast implementation based on the RTP protocol (shown in Listing 9.6b). Before the expiration date, the policy is changed to a service offering the "old" multicast implementation *and* the new one based on the RTMP protocol as shown in Listing 9.6c. When the temporal policy expires, it renews itself and the communication policy. Now, the communication policy supports both protocols for the next month as specified in the `duration` tag (P1M = period 1 Month) to allow compatibility for old clients. At the end of this month, the policy is changed again to the policy shown in Listing 9.6d. As soon as the temporal policy expires, the communication policy and the temporal policy are renewed. Now, the communication policy only supports the RTMP-based multicast implementation. Old clients are no longer supported. The service changes its protocol dependencies by changing the communication policy.

For the interaction with the Flash-based video-on-demand streaming, a first prototype of the Service-enabled Mashup Editor was used. The mashup editor was created with Adobe Flex. A Flex component (shown in Figure 9.16) was built as an interface for YouTube, allowing to click on an image preview of the search results to play this video in a `Player` component, as shown in Figure 9.17.

A user can easily use the YouTube component to watch videos inside the Mashup Editor. The next step is to provide components to convert the flv video format to MPEG video and then use the video face detector service.

9.6 Summary

In this chapter, a service-oriented infrastructure for multimedia processing using BPEL has been presented. Hence, the developed multimedia services can be easily integrated into existing business processes. To efficiently model the data flow in BPEL, Flex-SwA's reference concept is used. With the presented

```
<temporalPolicy name="http://fb12.de/vodTP"
 xmlns="http://fb12.de/2007/09/temporalpolicy">
 <expires>2009-04-01T00:00:00</expires>
 <onExpiration>
  <renew ref="http://fb12.de/vodTP">
    <duration>P1M</duration>
  </renew>
  <renew ref="http://fb12.de/vodCP">
    <duration>P1M</duration>
  </renew>
 </onExpiration>
</temporalPolicy>
```
                              (a)

```
<wsp:Policy Name="http://fb12.de/vodCP">
  <wsp:ExactlyOne>
    <cp:protocol name="rtp" operationref="streamVideo"
      protocolID="RTPv2"/>
  <wsp:ExactlyOne>
</wsp:Policy>
```
                              (b)

```
<wsp:Policy Name="http://fb12.de/vodCP">
  <wsp:ExactlyOne>
    <cp:protocol name="rtp" operationref="streamVideo"
      protocolID="RTPv2"/>
    <cp:protocol name="rtmp" operationref="streamVideo"
      protocolID="http://www.adobe.com/devnet/rtmp/"/>
  <wsp:ExactlyOne>
</wsp:Policy>
```
                              (c)

```
<wsp:Policy Name="http://fb12.de/vodCP">
  <wsp:ExactlyOne>
    <cp:protocol name="rtmp" operationref="streamVideo"
      protocolID="http://www.adobe.com/devnet/rtmp/"/>
  <wsp:ExactlyOne>
</wsp:Policy>
```
                              (d)

Listing 9.6: Temporal policy describing communication policies for a video-on-demand Service.

9.6. Summary

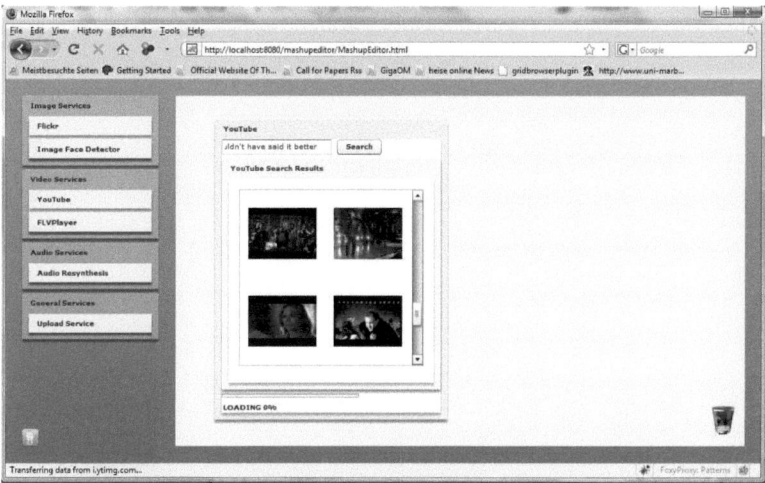

Figure 9.16: Screenshot of the Flex YouTube component.

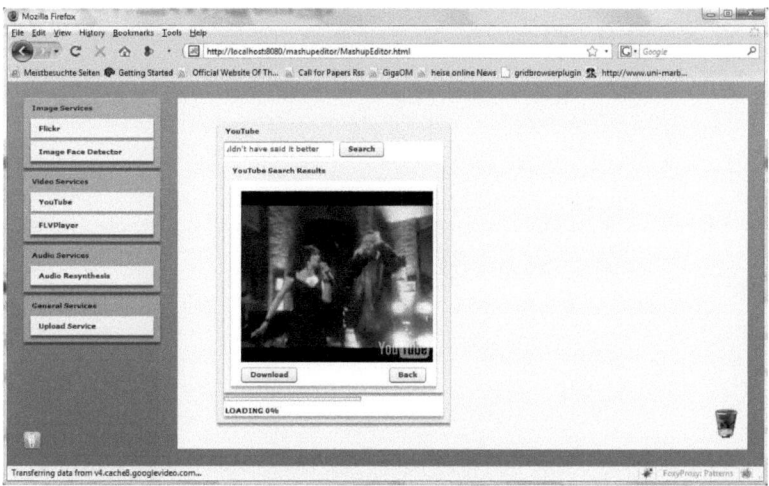

Figure 9.17: Screenshot of the Flex YouTube player component.

Web and Grid Service Browser and the Service-enabled Mashup Editor, users can easily use services of the SOA and can partially combine existing services and popular web applications to new services. To provide a scalable infrastructure, services can dynamically be added by leveraging Amazon's EC2. By using the Visual Grid Orchestrator, service developers can easily create new services by combining existing ones. A communication policy allows services to express protocol requirements regarding file transfers, streaming, or soft real-time. The evaluation of three use cases has demonstrated the feasibility of the proposed approaches.

Flex-SwA provides more efficiency for data transfers than SOAP and SOAP Messages with Attachments when configured with the correct communication patterns. It was shown that the overlapping of service execution and data transmission as well as the concurrent handling of data transfers leads to better performance. Flex-SwA is well suited for the transfer of bulk data in multimedia environments, as demonstrated for the audio resynthesis service.

The streaming capabilities of Flex-SwA speeded up the analysis. Two approaches to model the data transmission of services have been described. In the reference approach, a service returns a SOAP message with a reference to the calling BPEL workflow instance that then delegates this message to the destined consuming services. The consumer can then pull the data directly from the producer. This modeling style reduces the amount of data that is delegated via the workflow engine from one to another service. The streaming approach uses the Flex-SwA reference system to build up communication channels directly between a set of services. In contrast to the first modeling style, the task of data exchange is totally decoupled from the BPEL workflow. The BPEL engine just chooses the partners that build a communication channel between them. This leads to a trade-off between fast execution and control of the flow. Some control might be regained via callbacks.

For scalability reasons, services can be "outsourced" to the Amazon EC2. The evaluation has shown that the High CPU instances of EC2 provide a similar performance to the regular computers used for the analysis. Hence, it is not too difficult to calculate how many additional hosts are needed when the load increases.

The Web and Grid Service Browser provides special result presentations for multimedia data to offer human users an easy way to see or hear the service results.

The evaluation of the video on demand service has shown that it is hard to integrate certain types of applications into a SOA due to real-time constraints, streaming requirements or large file transfers. In case of the video-on-demand application, sending RTP packages over SOAP is too inefficient to allow a user to still watch the video. The delay between the packages becomes too big. With the help of a communication policy, requirements of the service can be described and thus services can be integrated into a SOA. For the interaction with the user,

9.6. Summary

the Service-enabled Mashup Editor provides a YouTube component as a frontend to the YouTube website. With this component, videos can be searched, selected and watched.

10
Related Work

The related work is divided into several areas:

- Description of temporal dimensions
- Definition of communication options for web services
- Facilitating flexible and efficient data handling
- Enabling simple service use
- Leveraging Grid resources for end user development
- Service-oriented multimedia analysis frameworks

10.1 Description of Temporal Dimensions

The WS-Agreement specification from October 2006 [16] defines the negotiation structure between a service consumer and a service provider to achieve an agreement on how a service is used, for example, with respect to service quality. The provider may offer capabilities, the consumer may suggest requirements that the provider can evaluate and then accept or reject. Although WS-Agreement identifies the problem that not all properties of a service can be described statically, it only offers an expiration time for an agreement, but no managing capabilities of dynamic properties of a service regarding actions that should be taken when an event occurs, such as the expiration of a policy.

Tian et al. [93] introduce a standardized way of describing QoS parameters for web services that enables the efficient, dynamic, and QoS-aware selection and monitoring of web services. They define a QoS XML Schema that describes QoS offerings and requirements. Dynamic properties cannot be described with this approach. Furthermore, temporal policies are applicable in a much broader area than only QoS.

Tosic et al. [94] extend WS-Policy by introducing WS-Policy4MASC. They define new types of policy assertions: goal, action, utility, and meta policy assertions. Goal policy assertions specify requirements or guarantees to be met (e.g., response time of an activity). Action policy assertions define actions to be taken as soon as certain conditions are met (e.g., if guarantees were not met). Examples of these actions are removal, addition, replacement, skipping, re-running of a sub-process, or process termination. Utility policy assertions specify how to bill the execution of an action. Meta-policy assertions are used to specify which action policy assertions are alternatives and which conflict resolution strategy should be used. The policy assertion types do not address the idea of describing dynamic properties. The defined actions are executed in the middleware, so they highly differ from an event/action mechanism for policy management. The temporal policy language could be used to add a temporal dimension to each of the different policy assertion types.

Liang et al. [67] introduce a policy framework for managing a customization policy. The service provider declares its customization capabilities. The service consumer proposes a customization request within the scope defined in the policy, receives an updated service description, and then invokes the updated service instance. The consumer is only able to modify the service's XML Schema types definition. The customization policy could make use of the temporal policy language to add a temporal dimension and thus provide explicit management capabilities of dynamic properties which then automatically result in the updated services depending on dynamic properties (instead of static properties).

Garcia et al. [43] present an approach to ease the selection of a web service based on non-functional properties, especially QoS properties. Their approach is based on WS-Policy and the Ontology Web Language (OWL) to enable a semantics-enriched description of QoS properties, i.e. the intersection of the requirements and capabilities is eased. The approach is not suitable to describe QoS properties that may vary over time, such as the response time. The temporal policy language could be used to extend the approach of Garcia et al.

10.2 Definition of Communication Options for Web Services

The WSDL 2.0 Recommendation of the W3C from June 2007 [27] allows to bind *endpoints* to other protocols than SOAP. It also defines three different message exchange patterns each of which consists of two messages at maximum. Additional MEPs are defined in the Working Group Note *Web Services Description Language*

10.2. Definition of Communication Options for Web Services 159

(WSDL) Version 2.0: Additional MEPs [66]. But these suffer from the same limitations, since they only allow to exchange one or two messages. The binding to other protocols than SOAP allows to *invoke* a service with protocols other than SOAP, but not to *communicate* with them after the invocation. The message exchange patterns are not suitable for more complex services with real-time or streaming requirements. Mechanisms from other web service specifications cannot easily be used with other protocols. With the help of the communication policy, however, it is possible to use SOAP to invoke a service and expose the protocol dependencies of the service via an embedded policy file.

The W3C Submission OWL-S by Martin et al. [70] is built on top of the Web Ontology Language (OWL) and introduces a `ServiceGrounding` providing information about the communication protocol the SOAP messages use. It uses the binding mechanism of WSDL. Although it explicitly states that other grounding mechanisms are possible, OWL-S concretely refers only to WSDL as a description for protocols, message formats, etc., which means that only SOAP is featured to invoke a service. Hence, it does not provide descriptive means to use other protocols besides SOAP to actually communicate with an application as the communication policy does.

The Service-Component Architecture (SCA) [56], introduced, among others, by BEA and IBM, provides a programming model to build applications based on a SOA. It focuses on the creation of service components as well as on the composition of existing services. It is possible to specify a binding that handles a conversation automatically besides the usual SOAP messages exchanged. A drawback is that bindings for existing applications have to be newly created. Some bindings are supported by default, e.g., JMS and EJB. The communication policy, however, allows the integration of complex applications by simply specifying a URI providing the necessary information for the protocol to use. Since the communication policy is based on WS-Policy, it can even be integrated into the SCA framework [57] that enables the usage of policies in combination with bindings (for example, a `SecurityPolicy` can be defined for the web service binding).

Approaches like Fast Web Services introduced by Sandoz et al. [85] reduce the size of the messages under loss of self-descriptiveness and human readability by using ASN.1 for the description of the SOAP envelope. Thus, the performance is improved. In applications where properties like self-descriptiveness and human readability are dispensable, this might be a good approach. However, by using a communication policy, these properties remain in the SOAP message used to trigger the communication with suitable protocols, such that it is not necessary to abandon these two characteristics of XML. Furthermore, a standardized means of describing that a service is a "Fast Web Service" are missing.

NaradaBrokering [40] is a powerful messaging substrate that internally uses events in a publish/subscribe manner for the communication. It provides access to JMS and JXTA networks, and implements the SOAP protocol as an interface to web and Grid services. In NaradaBrokering, every message is encapsulated in an event. If the message is leaving the Narada network, i.e. it is sent to a node not capable of NaradaBrokering functionality, it has first to be decapsulated. To provide multimedia capabilities, Narada uses special RTP events. Although a broker allows a non-web service component's request to be converted to a SOAP request, it does not use WSDL to describe its capabilities. This is because NaradaBrokering originates from audio/video conferencing. Its strength lies not in the description of services as required by a SOA, but in the delivery of messages via its powerful messaging substrate. Thus, NaradaBrokering's descriptive strength could perhaps be improved by leveraging the communication policy introduced in this thesis.

10.3 Facilitating Flexible and Efficient Data Handling

There are several approaches leading to more flexibility and better performance in SOAs compared to standard SOAP.

Allcock et al. [9] introduce GridFTP as a high performance data transfer protocol. GridFTP starts an extra process to efficiently transfer data from one node to another. It is completely decoupled from the service. The decoupling from the service violates the idea of service-orientation, since the data transfers are handled in a way not described in a standardized manner by the service interface. The Flex-SwA framework allows to couple the data transfer and service invocation again while still using efficient protocols for the data transfer.

Reliable File Transfer (RFT) [11] is a front-end Grid service that executes GridFTP. RFT is service-oriented but lacks the flexibility of dynamically transferring data during data production or service execution. Integrating the RFT capabilities into a Grid service or a client is a very hard task for a service developer. Using Flex-SwA's data transfer and integration capabilities considerably simplifies the development of services and clients.

OGSADAI [17] provides services to access data from different sources like databases, files, and so on. Data services can be used completely decoupled from other services. In contrast to OGSADAI, the Flex-SwA architecture allows to integrate the data transfer into the service invocation.

NaradaBrokering, as mentioned in the previous section, is a powerful messaging substrate based on the publish/subscribe paradigm and supports several protocols in which it can transport SOAP messages. However, NaradaBrokering does not allow to select an efficient protocol to transport bulk data and still use a SOAP message to invoke the service.

One reason for the bad performance of SOAP is the serialization (or deserialization) process, respectively. Abu-Ghazaleh et al. present an approach named differential serialization that reuses a serialized SOAP message as a template for further messages [6]. Furthermore, an approach to improve deserialization called differential deserialization is discussed [5]. Since transferring large amounts of data over SOAP is avoided when using the Flex-SwA architecture, the performance loss resulting from the serialization and deserialization of large amounts of data is circumvented, too. When the size of the required XML markup grows, these approaches can be used in addition to Flex-SwA to further improve the performance.

Ying et al. [98] show that pure SOAP produces too much overhead to be considered efficient and measure the performance of SOAP Messages with Attachments (SwA) [20]. The results of Ying et al. and Engelen et al. [95] show that SwA is significantly faster than SOAP when the amount of data increases. As an alternative to SwA, Seshasayee et al. introduce SOAP-bin and SOAP-binQ as a combination of SOAP with an efficient binary protocol [88]. SwA as well as SOAP-bin and SOAP-binQ suffer from the fact that the order of the transmission of data units (or attachments in SwA terms) cannot be chosen and overlapping of service execution and data transmission is not possible.

Nielsen et al. present an alternative to MIME (which is used as message format for SOAP Messages with Attachments) named Direct Internet Message Encapsulation (DIME) [82]. DIME enables random access to each message part of a multipart message.

To increase efficiency, Lu et al. present an implementation of a generic SOAP engine that supports textual and binary XML as encoding scheme of messages [69]. The problem is that the order of the data units transmission cannot be chosen and an overlapping of service execution and data transmission is not possible.

None of the approaches introduced in this section allows to configure services with different communication patterns that allow a flexible handling of data transfers. Only DIME can be used to also provide overlapping of service execution and data transmission but needs more implementation effort. Furthermore, none of these approaches allows to send data to a service after its invocation (post-invocation parameter transmission).

Koulouzis et al. [63] published an approach that allows to transfer large amounts of data as well as data streaming with a reference system in 2008. This approach is very similar to the already published Flex-SwA and post-invocation parameter transmission papers from 2006. However, it does not allow the configuration of communication patterns.

10.4 Enabling Simple Service Use

To simply use services in a familiar environment, a browser-based service invocation is desirable.

Gemstone [21] is an application based on the Mozilla Application Framework [75] and XULRunner [76] that allows users to browse a set of web services and enables dynamic integration of the user interface elements. The service providers have to specify the service and user interface. Gemstone is used to select services from a proprietary repository. Hence, Gemstone lacks a real browser integration. It only provides the integration of web services for which visualization code is written in XUL and JavaScript. This limits the use of Gemstone to service providers offering visualization code to their services and using the proprietary repository format supported by Gemstone. Since Gemstone is built on top of the Mozilla Framework, it only supports Transport Layer Security (TLS) and PKCS12 certificates. The lack of proxy certificate support considerably limits its use in Grid environments. Gemstone strictly supports client-side processing. For slow clients, it would be better if an option for server-side processing was available.

Web and Grid portals like GridSphere [92] provide access to a collection of services and a set of tools such as single-sign on, data management, and certificate management or collaboration capabilities (sharing, interlinking, and integrating multi-disciplinary datasets) like the GEON portal [78] directly through the browser. However, in order to operate portals, maintenance and administration efforts are needed. Furthermore, for each new service to add to the portal, a portlet has to be written.

The Web Services Remote Portlet (WSRP) specification [64] addresses part of the problem. A user interface defined at a remote site can be included in the portal. Still, each provider has to define the user interface for each of its service descriptions on the web or in a repository.

The Virtual Resource Browser (VBrowser) [83] tries to make the Grid more accessible to end users. It allows easy access to a number of high level services like RFT, a job submission service, Image Analysis, etc. The VBrowser is a standalone application and not integrated into a browser. But more importantly, it can not be used to invoke services that have not been integrated into the application. Whereas the Web and Grid Service Browser generates the user interface on the fly, the VBrowser can only access services that its developers integrated programmatically into it. Therefore, the Web and Grid Service Browser is much more adaptable and flexible.

Table 10.1 shows a detailed classification of the capabilities of the proposed Web and Grid Service Browser, of portals and of Gemstone for several criteria.

The capabilities of the browser extension, of portals, and of Gemstone can be classified by criteria like the quality of the integration into the web browser, the installation effort, the ease of use, the functionality, whether processing takes place locally or on service-side, the supported security level, GridFTP support and the supported types of certificates.

- **Integration:** The Web and Grid Service Browser Extension as well as

10.4. Enabling Simple Service Use

Table 10.1: Overview of the capabilities of the browser extension, portals, and Gemstone.

criteria	Web and Grid Service Browser Extension	Portals (like Gridsphere)	Gemstone
integration	direct browser integration	direct browser integration	new application based on Mozilla XULRunner
installation	Installation as simple as installing a Firefox extension	complete Globus Toolkit installation including myproxy-server and GridFTP Portlet	Installation as simple as installing a web browser
ease of use	arbitrary WSDL file is used to generate GUI	each service to be integrated into portal	WSDL only usable if in proprietary repository format *and* XUL and JavaScript has been written for it
functionality	Grid and Web Services	Grid and Web Services	Web Services
processing	local and server-side processing possible	server-side processing	local processing
security level	GSI support	GSI support	only https
GridFTP support	can be added by Firefox extension TOPAZ	yes	Firefox extension TOPAZ can be used separately with Firefox
certificates	proxy certificates	proxy certificates	"ordinary" certificates

portals like GridSphere provide a direct integration into the web browser, whereas Gemstone is a new application based on Mozilla XULRunner.

- **Installation:** The installation of the Web and Grid Service Browser Extension is as easy as installing Firefox extensions, namely via Drag&Drop. A portal needs a completely installed Globus Toolkit including a *myproxy-*server and the GridFTP Portlet. The complete Globus Toolkit requires a Unix operating system. The installation of Gemstone is comparable to the installation of a web browser.

- **Ease of use:** The Web and Grid Service Browser browses to the location of an arbitrary WSDL file to generate the GUI via which the service described by the WSDL document can be invoked, whereas for each service to be integrated into the portal, a portlet and a client have to be written. In Gemstone, only WSDL documents can be used if they have been stored in a proprietary repository format *and* if the application developer has deposited XUL and JavaScript code which is then executed by the Mozilla application.

- **Functionality:** The Web and Grid Service Browser and portals like GridSphere support Grid and web services whereas Gemstone only supports web services.

- **Processing:** The processing can take place either locally on the client or on service side. The Web and Grid Service Browser supports both modes depending on whether local or remote UI generators, execution engines and result presentation engines are used. Portals only support service side processing, Gemstone supports local processing.

- **Security Level:** The Web and Grid Service Browser and portals like GridSphere support the Grid Security Infrastructure (GSI). Gemstone only supports Transport Layer Security via https.

- **GridFTP support:** Portals like GridSphere support GridFTP. Gemstone and the Web and Grid Service Browser need the TOPAZ Firefox extension to add GridFTP functionality.

- **Certificates:** Portals like GridSphere and the Web and Grid Service Browser are able to use proxy certificates that are usually utilized when invoking a secured Grid service. Gemstone only makes use of ordinary certificates.

10.5 Leveraging Grid Resources for End User Development

Up to now, only few research efforts have been undertaken to leverage Grid and Cloud resources in the context of mashups. Approaches based on EzWeb/Fast by Lizcano et al. [68] deal—among others—with the adaptability of business processes to changing environmental situations in the context of mashups.

Nestler [79] proposes to use mashups as a means of communication between services and users. Simple mashups defined by end users are clearly separated from the complex development of workflows and business process integration. Existing services of a SOA should be usable as part of a mashup.

Björnstad et al. [22] propose a layered mashup architecture that cleanly separates the user interface from the integration logic and the data source providers.

None of the approaches above deal with the integration of Grid or Cloud resources into the mashup or mashup editor, respectively. Lizcano et al. even only deal with RESTful web services that are not suited for an integration into existing business processes. Björnstad et al. also do not take web services into account. The Service-enabled Mashup Editor presented in this thesis supports the use of web and Grid services for computationally demanding tasks and the combination of services with web applications.

Furthermore, there are already several popular tools available on the web.

Yahoo Pipes (`http://pipes.yahoo.com/pipes`) is a mashup editor that is mainly data driven. It is possible to combine data feeds to new RSS feeds via a visual editor. Yahoo Pipes is easy to use but a user cannot work directly with a result, since the result is an RSS feed.

Microsoft Popfly Mashup Creator (`http://www.popfly.com/mashupcreator`) is a visual editor based on Microsoft Silverlight offering reusable blocks that can be interconnected. Blocks can process input data of other blocks or even be games written with Silverlight. Even web services can be used. Although the functionality is extensive, one of the main problems is that Popfly is not a tool that can easily be used to create new applications, particularly not by computer novices.

Intel Mash Maker (`http://mashmaker.intel.com/web/`) provides an environment based on the web site a user visits with his/her browser. The web pages can be annotated and enriched by widgets that process the annotated information from the web pages. Again, this tool is very useful but is hard for computer novices to use.

Since most of the editors are hard to use for computer novices, the Service-enabled Mashup Editor presented in this thesis provides two views, one for the developer and one for the user. The user view is designed to provide a more restricted functionality that is more easy to use. The developer view, however, provides the full functionality. Furthermore, the other editors do not leverage high performance computing resources such as Grid or Cloud resources.

10.6 Frameworks for Service-oriented Multimedia Analysis

The CASSANDRA framework [80] is a distributed multimedia content analysis system that is based on a service-oriented architecture and aims to facilitate the composition of applications from distributed components on a network of cooperating devices (like PC or consumer electronics equipment). The individual analysis components are encapsulated into functional units, called Service Units. All units on one particular device are managed by a local component repository that is synchronized by a master repository. Service composition is initiated by a special coordination component. Each Service Unit has a control and a data streaming interface. The control interface is based on UPnP, while the streaming interface is based on TCP/IP. This framework does not use web services to build a SOA, neither for the service definition nor for workflow composition; it uses UPnP. Since service composition is performed by a special component, the above mentioned coordination component is just used to setup the workflow. In general, this framework is similar to the streaming approach proposed in this thesis, but does neither leverage the expressiveness of BPEL nor the flexibility of Flex-SwA. The data transport is fixed to TCP/IP, whereas the use of Flex-SwA allows the use of custom protocols, e.g., RFT, GridFTP, HTTP or UDP. The use of UPnP may be useful for controlling consumer electronics, but is critical in terms of security and will probably not find a broad adoption by network administrators.

Barker et al. [19] present an architecture and an API to support a distributed data flow model in conjunction with a centralized control flow. To provide a non-centralized data flow from one service to another service, the authors make use of proxies that are responsible for data management and service invocation. The proxies are placed near the service that they administrate. A service invocation has to be passed over a proxy, the produced data is saved through the proxy and a reference to this data is delegated back to the calling centralized workflow engine. This solution does not directly support WSRF-based services that are often more suited for multimedia content analysis tasks. Although this approach leads to a distributed data flow with reduced data movement, it also introduces an additional indirection stage for service calls. Since the proxies should be placed on the same web server or domain and the reference system needs to store the service results on local disk, a resource competition between service and proxies may occur.

Zeng et al. [100] present an approach for avoiding a centralized data transmission in BPEL-based workflows in terms of Grid computing. They distinguish between intra-workflow and inter-workflow data communication. While the first

10.6. Frameworks for Service-oriented Multimedia Analysis   167

model focuses on direct data transmission between two services in one workflow, the second model also covers data transmission between several Grid workflows. Both models make use of two special Grid services. In the case of intra workflows, a so-called data transmission factory service is called from the workflow engine to set up a data transmission service that handles the direct data transfer from one Grid service to another and notifies the status to the engine. The workflow engine just handles control messages and small data packages. To support this kind of data transmission through BPEL, a new language element called `<dataTransmission>` has been defined. It specifies source and target service and transport type, which can be GridFTP or notifications. In the inter-workflow case, a so-called data proxy service (DPS) is used to manage the data transport between different Grid workflows and/or services. The DPS is part of the workflow engine and has the same lifetime as the corresponding workflow. In contrast to the previous approach, this proposal is specialized for Grid services and does not support "normal" web services. Since BPEL is extended with an additional element, it is not conforming to the standard; workflows cannot be executed on standard BPEL engines. Furthermore, in the case of inter-workflow data transfers, a specially adopted workflow engine must be used for the DPS instances.

Blower et al. [24] have developed a system for creating a new service type called Styx Grid Service (SGS). The system wraps command-line programs and allows them to be run over the Internet. It is based on a Java implementation of the file-sharing protocol Styx and allows data streaming from service to service over transport protocols like TCP/IP or UDP. A SGS can be used in a web service or WSRF environment. An orchestration into workflows is also possible through simple shell scripts or graphical workflow system like the Taverna workbench (http://taverna.sourceforge.net/). In contrast to SGS, the proposed multimedia SOA is based on the de-facto standard for business workflows, namely BPEL, and can thus be integrated into business processes. The granularity of the SGS is very coarse, since a SGS can only wrap whole executables. The proposed multimedia SOA works on web or Grid service level, i.e. on methods or functions.

11
Conclusions and Future Work

11.1 Summary

This thesis has shown how WS-Policies can be used to enhance web services in the areas of temporal dimensions, streaming, real-time, and file transfers. With the addition of temporal policies, the management of WS-Policies is possible and enables, for example, strategies to switch protocol dependencies of services. The protocol dependencies can be described by a communication policy that allows services to express protocol requirements regarding streaming, real-time, or file transfers. On top of the policy descriptions, new mechanisms and approaches have been designed to alleviate efficient and flexible data handling, usability, and to even allow the involvement of the end user in the development process. The Flex-SwA architecture allows the flexible handling of data by providing several communication patterns. Efficient file transfers can be described by a communication policy and executed by the Flex-SwA framework. With the Web and Grid Service Browser, a web-based concept for a generic web and Grid service client (and its implementation) has been introduced that simplifies the use of web and Grid services. Here, the communication policy provides the means to integrate efficient data transfers based on Flex-SwA into the service invocation. The concept of the Web and Grid Service Browser is extensible for different mime types. For multimedia data, special plugins have been designed that allow listening to audio, watching video, and grouping images. To involve the end user in the development process, a Service-enabled Mashup Editor has been presented allowing the end user to develop new applications by combining existing web and Grid services with popular web applications. Again, the communication policy provides descriptive means for file transfers and Flex-SwA references are used for the actual data transmission.

The evaluation has shown how a multimedia SOA can be built with the concepts presented in this thesis. The temporal policy has enabled the switching of the required multicast protocol for a video-on-demand service. The communication policy has described the protocols via which the Flex-SwA framework communicated when file transfers or streaming was required. In these areas, Flex-SwA has provided more efficient means of communication than standard mechanisms like SOAP or SOAP Messages with Attachments. The invocation of multimedia services and the result presentation of the Web and Grid Service Browser has been presented for an audio resynthesis service and a video face detection service. The Service-enabled Mashup Editor has provided—among other components—a simple Flash Player to consume the new multicast protocol that has been used after the protocol switch.

11.2 Future Work

There are several areas for future work.

A fine-grained policy weaving for temporal policies will be investigated. The implementation of the Temporal Policy Runtime Environment will be extended by a independent validator component. By exposing the temporal policies like other policies or WSDL descriptions, the policies can be used to support client-side decisions. For example, if temporal policies are used to describe the validity period of prices for resources, it is possible to develop client-side strategies for buying resources (e.g., as described by Buyya et al. [26]).

The communication policy could be further extended by adding descriptive power to the communication policy, so that a client generation based on platform requirements is possible. Additionally, virtualization technologies could be investigated to securely execute the installation of client software without harming other users or the operating system. Independent of the web services area, the communication policy could be adapted to extend the descriptive means for popular web applications used in mashups. For example, Flickr works with specific encodings to specify the format/parameters of the HTTP response. This could be described by a communication policy.

The Flex-SwA implementation will be evaluated in more detail. Tests of the WebVoice service will be performed on different hardware. These tests will help to evaluate which communication patterns are especially useful for which hardware (dual-core, single-core, etc.). For the face detection service, the suitable number of frames per reference to attain a good balance between data flow control and efficiency will be investigated.

For the Web and Grid Service Browser, a notification system is planned for the future to allow the invocation of services in an asynchronous way. Furthermore, the support of REST services is intended. An investigation of complex visualizations with the help of Java3D is planned. Finally, an evaluation of the

11.2. Future Work

functionality in further use cases will be performed.

For the Service-enabled Mashup Editor, the development of new components is planned. The next components to be added are a Flash to MPEG converter and a shot boundary detection service for videos. Both components allow the analysis of YouTube videos, such that a preview (or summary) of the video can be created based on the MPEG-7 output of the shot boundary detection service. To achieve a convergence of mashups and workflows, a creation of BPEL workflows from the mashup components is planned. The BPEL workflows could be enriched by graphical information for a representation in a mashup editor. In this way, both are possible—the use of the mashup for end users and the headless use of workflows that can be integrated into business processes.

List of Figures

1.1	Overview of WS-Standards.	3
1.2	Roles in a service-oriented environment relating to services.	8
2.1	Component overview.	16
3.1	Overview: Temporal Policy.	21
3.2	Dependency tree for several WS-TemporalPolicies and WS-Policies.	28
3.3	Functional components of the temporal policy runtime environment.	30
3.4	States of a policy.	31
4.1	Overview: Communication Policy.	33
4.2	Application without SOA integration.	34
4.3	Application wrapped by a service.	35
4.4	Application realized as services.	36
4.5	Fully integrated application.	39
5.1	Overview: Flex-SwA.	47
5.2	An example of a SOAP RPC.	49
5.3	General web service interaction pattern using SwA.	51
5.4	The Flex-SwA protocol stack.	52
5.5	Example of stream-based production/consumption of parameters.	54
5.6	Sequential and pipelined processing.	55
5.7	Communication patterns in Flex-SwA.	58
5.8	Reduced data movement and seamless message forwarding.	61
6.1	Overview: Web and Grid Service Browser.	63
6.2	Invoking a service from the Web and Grid Service Browser.	68
7.1	Overview: Service-enabled Mashup Editor.	73
7.2	Overview of the Service-enabled Mashup Editor.	76
8.1	Message processing in Apache Axis (see Graham et al. [45]). . . .	82
8.2	Policy weaving.	86
8.3	Middleware components of Flex-SwA.	90

8.4	Protocol capabilities for transferring large amounts of data and PIPT.	91
8.5	Buffers used in Flex-SwA.	92
8.6	Threads used in Flex-SwA.	94
8.7	Interaction between the components of Flex-SwA.	95
8.8	User interface of the search engine.	108
8.9	Result of a Grid service search.	109
8.10	Screenshot of the Service-enabled Mashup Editor.	114
9.1	General roles in a multimedia SOA.	121
9.2	Multimedia analysis procedure.	122
9.3	Data flow via a BPEL4WS engine.	124
9.4	Layer model for a multimedia SOA.	127
9.5	Average processing time of the `wav2splice` operation.	136
9.6	Standard deviation for invoking the `wav2splice` operation.	136
9.7	Client-side heap space consumption.	137
9.8	Analysis runtimes for 20051227_125800_CNN_LIVEFROM_ENG.	138
9.9	Analysis runtimes for 20051209_125800_CNN_LIVEFROM_ENG.	139
9.10	Process runtimes in a virtualized environment.	141
9.11	Screenshot of Firefox showing a WSDL file.	146
9.12	Screenshot of the `WebVoice` service user unterface.	147
9.13	Result of the `wav2splice` operation.	148
9.14	Screenshot of the results of the face detection workflow service for a Meat Loaf music video.	149
9.15	Screenshot of the face detection workflow in ViGO.	150
9.16	Screenshot of the Flex YouTube component.	153
9.17	Screenshot of the Flex YouTube player component.	153

List of Tables

3.1	Overview of event handlers in temporal policies.	27
3.2	Overview of actions in temporal policies.	27
4.1	Overview of the communication policy.	45
8.1	Protocols supported by Flex-SwA and their corresponding namespaces.	100
9.1	Average time for preparing transmission and reception of a multimedia stream.	142
9.2	Standard deviation for preparing transmission and reception of a multimedia stream.	143
9.3	Average time for preparing transmission and reception of a multimedia stream.	144
10.1	Overview of the capabilities of the browser extension, portals, and Gemstone.	163

Listings

3.1	Example of a WS-Policy using `ExactlyOne`.	23
3.2	Example of a WS-Policy using `All`.	23
3.3	XML schema for a temporal policy (part I).	24
3.4	XML schema for a temporal policy (part II).	25
3.5	Example of a temporal policy using the `expires` element.	26
3.6	Example of a temporal policy using the `startTime` and `endTime` elements.	26
3.7	Example of a temporal policy that affects other temporal policies.	29
3.8	Example of a policy that exposes a validity date.	31
4.1	Policy for a real-time service.	39
4.2	Link to a sophisticated client.	41
4.3	Link to a sophisticated client specifying requirements.	42
4.4	Communication policy for a data service.	43
5.1	Example of a MIME multipart/related message.	50
5.2	XML schema for the Flex-SwA reference.	56
8.1	Modified Apache Axis `web.xml`.	87
8.2	Axis service description including a reference to the communication policy.	88
8.3	Axis service description including information for the communication policy.	89
8.4	Implementation of a JSON outport.	93
8.5	`WebVoice` client using the `Flex-SwA Call`.	96
8.6	Implementation of a JSON inport.	98
8.7	Example `flexswa.properties` file.	99
8.8	Running multiple servers.	99
8.9	Example of a deployment descriptor for Flex-SwA.	99
8.10	Structure of the `observe` function.	102
8.11	Structure of the `stream converter` component.	103
8.12	Initialization of the Java Bridge.	105
8.13	Assigning an identifier to each browser tab.	107
8.14	Executing a WSRF-query from Java.	107

8.15	Return Message for a WSRF-Query (namespaces left out).	108
8.16	Schematic representation of the `wav2splice` operation.	111
8.17	Definition of the editor layout.	115
8.18	Placing components on the canvas.	116
8.19	Switching from user view to developer view.	116
9.1	Implementation of the `wav2splice` operation (exception handling omitted).	133
9.2	Implementation of the lazy nonblocking variant of the `wav2splice` operation (exception handling omitted).	134
9.3	Implementation of the `wav2splice` operation with SwA (exception handling omitted).	135
9.4	Dynamic invokehandler within the BPEL process.	140
9.5	Policy embedded in WSDL for a simple video-on-demand service.	144
9.6	Temporal policy describing communication policies for a video-on-demand Service.	152

Bibliography

[1] Web Services Interoperability. http://www.ws-i.org/.

[2] XStream. http://xstream.codehaus.org/.

[3] H.323 : Packet-based Multimedia Communications Systems, 2006. http://www.itu.int/rec/T-REC-H.323-200606-I/en.

[4] Web Services Notification (WSN) 1.3, October 2006. http://www.oasis-open.org/committees/tc_home.php?wg_abbrev=wsn.

[5] Nayef Abu-Ghazaleh and Michael J. Lewis. Differential Deserialization for Optimized SOAP Performance. In *Proc. of the Int'l. Conference for High Performance Computing, Networking, and Storage*, page 21, 2005.

[6] Nayef Abu-Ghazaleh, Michael J. Lewis, and Madhusudhan Govindaraju. Differential Serialization for Optimized SOAP Performance. In *Proc. of the 13th IEEE Int'l. Symposium on High Performance Distributed Computing*, pages 55–64, 2004.

[7] Adobe. RTMP Specification, 2009. http://www.adobe.com/devnet/rtmp/.

[8] Eyhab Al-Masri and Qusay H. Mahmoud. Investigating Web Services on the World Wide Web. In *WWW '08: Proceeding of the 17th International Conference on World Wide Web*, pages 795–804, New York, NY, USA, 2008. ACM.

[9] W. Allcock, J. Bester, J. Bresnahan, A. Chervenak, I. Foster, C. Kesselman, S. Meder, V. Nefedova, D. Quesnel, and S. Tuecke. Data Management and Transfer in High Performance Computational Grid Environments. *Parallel Computing Journal*, Vol. 28 (5):749–771, May 2002.

[10] W. Allcock, J. Bester, J. Bresnahan, S. Meder, P. Plaszczak, and S. Tuecke. GridFTP: Protocol Extensions to FTP for the Grid. GFD-R-P.020 (Proposed Recommendation), April 2003.

[11] William E. Allcock, Ian Foster, and Ravi Madduri. Reliable Data Transport: A Critical Service for the Grid. In *Building Service Based Grids Workshop, Global Grid Forum 11*, 2004.

[12] Amazon Web Services LLC. Amazon Elastic Compute Cloud (EC2). http://aws.amazon.com/ec2/.

[13] Amazon Web Services LLC. Amazon Simple Storage Service (S3). http://aws.amazon.com/s3/.

[14] Steve Anderson, Jeff Bohren, Toufic Boubez, and Marc Chanliau. Web Services Secure Conversation Language (WS-SecureConversation), February 2005. http://specs.xmlsoap.org/ws/2005/02/sc/WS-SecureConversation.pdf.

[15] Tony Andrews, Francisco Curbera, Hitesh Dholakia, Yaron Goland, Johannes Klein, Frank Leymann, Kevin Liu, Dieter Roller, Doug Smith, Satish Thatte, Ivana Trickovic, and Sanjiva Weerawarana. Business Process Execution Language for Web Services version 1.1, 2003. http://www-128.ibm.com/developerworks/library/specification/ws-bpel/.

[16] Alain Andrieux, Karl Czajkowski, Asit Dan, Kate Keahey, Heiko Ludwig, Toshiyuki Nakata, Jim Pruyne, John Rofrano, Steve Tuecke, and Ming Xu. Web Services Agreement Specification (WS-Agreement), October 2006.

[17] Mario Antonioletti, Neil P. Chue Hong, Alastair C. Hume, Mike Jackson, Kostas Karasavvas, Amy Krause, Jennifer M. Schopf, Malcolm P. Atkinson, Bartosz Dobrzelecki, Malcolm Illingworth, Nicola McDonnell, Mark Parsons, and Elias Theocharopoulos. OGSA-DAI 3.0 - The Whats and the Whys. In *Proceedings of the UK e-Science All Hands Meeting*, pages 158–165, 2007.

[18] Keith Ballinger, David Ehnebuske, Christopher Ferris, Martin Gudgin, Canyang Kevin Liu, Mark Nottingham, and Prasad Yendluri. WS-I Basic Profile, April 2006. http://www.ws-i.org/Profiles/BasicProfile-1.1.html.

[19] Adam Barker, Jon B. Weissman, and Jano van Hemert. Orchestrating Data-Centric Workflows. In *Proc. of the 8th IEEE International Symposium on Cluster Computing and the Grid (CCGRID '08)*, pages 210–217. IEEE Computer Society, 2008.

[20] John J. Barton, Satish Thatte, and Henrik Frystyk Nielsen. SOAP Messages with Attachments. W3C Note, 2000. http://www.w3.org/TR/SOAP-attachments.

[21] Karan Bhatia, Brent Stearn, Michela Taufer, Richard Zamudio, and Daniel Catarino. Extending Grid Protocols onto the Desktop using the Mozilla Framework. In *2nd International Workshop on Grid Computing Environments (GCE 2006)*, pages 1–8, November 2006.

[22] Biörn Biörnstad and Cesare Pautasso. *Let It Flow: Building Mashups with Data Processing Pipelines*, chapter Mashups, pages 15–28. Springer-Verlag, Berlin, Heidelberg, 2009.

[23] Paul V. Biron and Ashok Malhotra. XML Schema Part 2: Datatypes Second Edition. Technical report, W3C, 2004.

[24] J. D. Blower, A. B. Harrison, and K. Haines. Styx Grid Services: Lightweight, Easy-to-Use Middleware for Scientific Workflows. In *International Conference on Computational Science (3)*, pages 996–1003, 2006.

[25] Russell Butek. Which style of WSDL should I use? IBM developer-Works, May 2005. http://www.ibm.com/developerworks/webservices/library/ws-whichwsdl/.

[26] Rajkumar Buyya and Sudharshan Vazhkudai. Compute Power Market: Towards a Market-Oriented Grid. In *The First IEEE/ACM International Symposium on Cluster Computing and the Grid (CCGrid)*, pages 574–581, 2001.

[27] Roberto Chinnici, Hugo Haas, Amelia A. Lewis, Jean-Jacques Moreau, David Orchard, and Sanjiva Weerawarana. Web Services Description Language (WSDL) Version 2.0 Part 2: Adjuncts, June 2007. http://www.w3.org/TR/2007/REC-wsdl20-adjuncts-20070626/.

[28] Roberto Chinnici, Jean-Jacques Moreau, Arthur Ryman, and Sanjiva Weerawarana. Web Services Description Language (WSDL) Version 2.0 Part 1: Core Language. Technical report, W3C, 2007.

[29] Erik Christensen, Francisco Curbera, Greg Meredith, and Sanjiva Weerawarana. Web Services Description Language (WSDL) 1.1. W3C Note, March 2001.

[30] Luc Clement, Andrew Hately, Claus von Riegen, and Tony Rogers. Universal Description Discovery & Integration (UDDI), 2004. http://uddi.org/pubs/uddi_v3.htm.

[31] Jos de Bruijn, Christoph Bussler, John Domingue, Dieter Fensel, Martin Hepp, Uwe Keller, Michael Kifer, Birgitta König-Ries, Jacek Kopecky, Rubén Lara, Holger Lausen, Eyal Oren, Axel Polleres, Dumitru Roman, James Scicluna, and Michael Stollberg. Web Service Modeling Ontology (WSMO), June 2005. http://www.w3.org/Submission/WSMO/.

[32] Giovanni Della-Libera, Martin Gudgin, Phillip Hallam-Baker, Maryann Hondo, Hans Granqvist, Chris Kaler, Hiroshi Maruyama, Michael McIntosh, Anthony Nadalin, Nataraj Nagaratnam, Rob Philpott, Hemma Prafullchandra, John Shewchuk, Doug Walter, and Riaz Zolfonoon. Web Services Security Policy Language (WS-SecurityPolicy), July 2005. http://www.ibm.com/developerworks/library/specification/ws-secpol/.

[33] Xin Dong, Alon Halevy, Jayant Madhavan, Ema Nemes, and Jun Zhang. Similarity Search for Web Services. In *30th International Conference on Very Large Data Bases (VLDB)*, pages 372–383. Morgan Kaufmann, 2004.

[34] T. Dörnemann, E. Juhnke, and B. Freisleben. On-Demand Resource Provisioning for Workflows Using Amazon's Elastic Compute Cloud. In *Proceedings of the 9th IEEE International Symposium on Cluster Computing and the Grid (CCGrid '09)*, page (to appear). IEEE Press, 2009.

[35] Tim Dörnemann, Thomas Friese, Sergej Herdt, Ernst Juhnke, and Bernd Freisleben. Grid Workflow Modelling Using Grid-Specific BPEL Extensions. In *Proceedings of the German e-Science Conference (GES)*, pages 1–8, 2007.

[36] Viktor S. Wold Eide, Frank Eliassen, Ole-Christoffer Granmo, and Olav Lysne. Scalable Independent Multi-level Distribution in Multimedia Content Analysis. In *Proceedings of the Joint International Workshops on Interactive Distributed Multimedia Systems and Protocols for Multimedia Systems (IDMS/PROMS)*, pages 37–48, London, UK, 2002. Springer-Verlag.

[37] Jeremy Elson and Jon Howell. Handling flash crowds from your garage. In *ATC'08: USENIX 2008 Annual Technical Conference*, pages 171–184, Berkeley, CA, USA, 2008. USENIX Association.

[38] Ian Foster, Carl Kesselman, and Steven Tuecke. The Anatomy of the Grid: Enabling Scalable Virtual Organizations. *The International Journal of High Performance Computing Applications*, 15(3):200–222, 2001.

[39] Ian T. Foster. Globus Toolkit Version 4: Software for Service-Oriented Systems. In *International Conference on Network and Parallel Computing (IFIP)*, volume 3779 of *Lecture Notes in Computer Science*, pages 2–13. Springer, 2005.

[40] Geoffrey Fox, Shrideep Pallickara, Marlon Pierce, and Harshawardhan Gadgil. Building Messaging Substrates for Web and Grid Applications. In *Philosophical Transactions of the Royal Society: Mathematical, Physical and Engineering Sciences. Volume 363, Number 1833.*, pages 1757–1773. IEEE, August 2005. http://www.naradabrokering.org/papers.htm.

BIBLIOGRAPHY 183

[41] N. Freed and N. Borenstein. RFC 2045: Multipurpose Internet Mail Extensions (MIME) Part One: Format of Internet Message Bodies, 1996. http://www.ietf.org/rfc/rfc2045.

[42] Thomas Friese, Matthew Smith, and Bernd Freisleben. GDT: A Toolkit for Grid Service Development. In *Proceedings of the 3rd International Conference on Grid Service Engineering and Management*, pages 131–148, 2006.

[43] Diego Zuquim Guimaraes Garcia and Maria Beatriz Felgar de Toledo. Semantics-enriched QoS Policies for Web Service Interactions. In *Proceedings of the 12th Brazilian Symposium on Multimedia and the Web (WebMedia)*, pages 35–44. ACM, 2006.

[44] C. Germain, V. Breton, P. Clarysse, Y. Gaudeau, T. Glatard, E. Jeannot, Y. Legre, C. Loomis, J. Montagnat, J.-M. Moureaux, A. Osorio, X. Pennec, and R. Texier. Grid-enabling Medical Image Analysis. In *Proceedings of the Fifth IEEE International Symposium on Cluster Computing and the Grid (CCGrid'05)*, volume 1, pages 487–495. IEEE Computer Society, 2005.

[45] Steve Graham, Doug Davis, Simeon Simeonov, Glen Daniels, Peter Brittenham, Yuichi Nakamura, Paul Fremantle, Dieter König, and Claudia Zentner. *Building Web Services with Java*, chapter 5, pages 236–250. Developer's Library, 2005.

[46] Steve Graham, Anish Karmarkar, Jeff Mischkinsky, Ian Robinson, Igor Sedukhin, Jem Treadwell, Latha Srinivasan, Tim Banks, Tom Maguire, David Snelling, Lily Liu, and Sam Meder. Web Services Resource Framework (WSRF), April 2006. http://www.oasis-open.org/committees/tc_home.php?wg_abbrev=wsrf.

[47] M. Gudgin, M. Hadley, N. Mendelsohn, J.-J. Moreau, and H. F. Nielsen. SOAP Version 1.2, Part 1: Messaging Framework, 2003.

[48] Martin Gudgin, Marc Hadley, and Tony Rogers. Web Services Addressing 1.0 - Core, 2006. http://www.w3.org/TR/ws-addr-core/.

[49] Martin Gudgin, Marc Hadley, Tony Rogers, and Ümit Yalçinalp. Web Services Addressing 1.0 – Metadata. Technical report, W3C, September 2007.

[50] Venkat N. Gudivada and Jagadeesh Nandigam. Enterprise Application Integration Using Extensible Web Services. In *ICWS '05: Proceedings of the IEEE International Conference on Web Services*, pages 41–48, Washington, DC, USA, 2005. IEEE Computer Society.

[51] S. Heinzl, M. Mathes, T. Stadelmann, D. Seiler, M. Diegelmann, H. Dohmann, and B. Freisleben. The Web Service Browser: Automatic Client Generation and Efficient Data Transfer for Web Services. In *Proc. of the 7th IEEE International Conference on Web Services (ICWS 2009)*, page (accepted for publication). IEEE Press, 2009.

[52] S. Heinzl, D. Seiler, E. Juhnke, T. Stadelmann, R. Ewerth, M. Grauer, and B. Freisleben. A Scalable Service-Oriented Architecture for Multimedia Analysis, Synthesis, and Consumption. *International Journal of Web and Grid Services*, Inderscience Publishers:(accepted for publication), 2009.

[53] Steffen Heinzl, Markus Mathes, and Bernd Freisleben. A Web Service Communication Policy for Describing Non-Standard Application Requirements. In *Proc. of the IEEE/IPSJ Symposium on Applications and the Internet (Saint 2008)*, pages 40–47. IEEE Computer Society Press, 2008.

[54] Steffen Heinzl, Markus Mathes, and Bernd Freisleben. The Grid Browser: Improving Usability in Service-Oriented Grids by Automatically Generating Clients and Handling Data Transfers. In *Proceedings of the Fourth IEEE International Conference on eScience*, pages 269–276. IEEE Press, 2008.

[55] Steffen Heinzl, Markus Mathes, Thomas Friese, Matthew Smith, and Bernd Freisleben. Flex-SwA: Flexible Exchange of Binary Data Based on SOAP Messages with Attachments. In *Proc. of the IEEE International Conference on Web Services, Chicago, USA*, pages 3–10. IEEE Press, 2006.

[56] IBM. Service Component Architecture Assembly Model Specification, 2007. http://www.osoa.org/display/Main/Service+Component+Architecture+Specifications.

[57] IBM. Service Component Architecture Policy Framework, 2007. http://www.osoa.org/display/Main/Service+Component+Architecture+Specifications.

[58] innoQ. Web services standards as of q1 2007, 2007. http://www.innoq.com/soa/ws-standards/poster/.

[59] Intel Corporation. OpenCV, 2008. http://www.intel.com/technology/computing/opencv/.

[60] F. Jammes and H. Smit. Service-Oriented Paradigms in Industrial Automation. *IEEE Transactions on Industrial Informatics*, 1:62–69, 2005.

[61] Mira Kajko-Mattsson, Grace A. Lewis, and Dennis B. Smith. A Framework for Roles for Development, Evolution and Maintenance of SOA-Based Systems. In *SDSOA '07: Proceedings of the International Workshop on Sys-*

tems Development in SOA Environments, page 7. IEEE Computer Society, 2007.

[62] Konstantinos Karasavvas, Mario Antonioletti, Malcolm Atkinson, Neil C. Hong, Tom Sugden, Alastair Hume, Mike Jackson, Amrey Krause, and Charaka Palansuriya. Introduction to OGSA-DAI Services. *Lecture Notes in Computer Science*, 3458:1–12, June 2005.

[63] Spiros Koulouzis, Edgar Meij, M. Scott Marshall, and Adam Belloum. Enabling Data Transport Between Web Services Through Alternative Protocols and Streaming. In *Proceedings of the Fourth IEEE International Conference on eScience*, pages 400–401, 2008.

[64] Alan Kropp, Carsten Leue, Rich Thompson, Chris Braun, Jeff Broberg, Mark Cassidy, Michael Freedman, Timothy N. Jones, Thomas Schaeck, and Gil Tayar. Web Services for Remote Portlets Specification. OASIS Standard, August 2003. http://www.oasis-open.org/committees/wsrp.

[65] Xuejia Lai and James L. Massey. A Proposal for a New Block Encryption Standard. *Lecture Notes in Computer Science*, 473:389, 1991.

[66] Amelia A. Lewis. Web Services Description Language (WSDL) Version 2.0: Additional MEPs, June 2007. http://www.w3.org/TR/2007/NOTE-wsdl20-additional-meps-20070626/.

[67] Haiqi Liang, Wei Sun, Xin Zhang, and Zhongbo Jiang. A Policy Framework for Collaborative Web Service Customization. In *Proceedings of the Second IEEE International Symposium on Service-Oriented System Engineering (SOSE)*, pages 197–204, 2006.

[68] David Lizcano, Javier Soriano, Marcos Reyes, and Juan J. Hierro. EzWeb/FAST: Reporting on a Successful Mashup-based Solution for Developing and Deploying Composite Applications in the Upcoming Web of Services. In *Proceedings of the 10th International Conference on Information Integration and Web-based Applications & Services*, pages 15–24, 2008.

[69] Wei Lu, Kenneth Chiu, and Dennis Gannon. Building a Generic SOAP Framework over Binary XML. In *Proc. of the 15th IEEE Int'l. Symposium on High Performance Distributed Computing*, pages 195–204, 2006.

[70] David Martin, Mark Burstein, Jerry Hobbs, Ora Lassila, Drew McDermott, Sheila McIlraith, Srini Narayanan, Massimo Paolucci, Bijan Parsia, Terry Payne, Evren Sirin, Naveen Srinivasan, and Katia Sycara. OWL-S: Semantic Markup for Web Services, 2004. http://www.w3.org/Submission/OWL-S/.

[71] Massachusetts Institute of Technology (MIT). Semantic Interoperability of Metadata and Information in unLike Environments (SIMILE). http://simile.mit.edu/.

[72] M. Mathes, S. Heinzl, and B. Freisleben. WS-TemporalPolicy: A WS-Policy Extension for Describing Service Properties with Time Constraints. In *Proceedings of the First IEEE International Workshop On Real-Time Service-Oriented Architecture and Applications (RTSOAA 2008) of the 32nd IEEE Computer Software and Applications Conference (COMPSAC 2008)*, pages 1180 – 1186. IEEE CS Press, 2008.

[73] M. Mathes, S. Heinzl, T. Friese, and B. Freisleben. Enabling Post-Invocation Parameter Transmission in Service-Oriented Environments. In *Proc. of the International Conference on Networking and Services, Silicon Valley, USA*, pages 55–60. IEEE Press, 2006.

[74] Nilo Mitra and Yves Lafon. SOAP Version 1.2, Part 0: Primer, 2007. http://www.w3.org/TR/soap12-part0/.

[75] Mozilla. Mozilla Application Framework. http://developer.mozilla.org/en/docs/Mozilla_Application_Framework_in_Detail.

[76] Mozilla. XULRunner. http://developer.mozilla.org/en/docs/XULRunner.

[77] Anthony Nadalin, Chris Kaler, Ronald Monzillo, and Phillip Hallam-Baker. Web Services Security: SOAP Message Security 1.1 5 (WS-Security 2004), OASIS Standard Specification, February 2006. http://www.oasis-open.org/committees/download.php/16790/wss-v1.1-spec-os-SOAPMessageSecurity.pdf.

[78] Ullas Nambia, Bertram Ludaescher, Kai Lin, and Chaitan Baru. The GEON Portal: Accelerating Knowledge Discovery in the Geosciences. In *8th ACM International Workshop on Web Information and Data Management (WIDM 2006)*, pages 83 – 90. ACM, November 2006.

[79] Tobias Nestler. Towards a Mashup-driven End-User Programming of SOA-based Applications. In *Proceedings of the 10th International Conference on Information Integration and Web-based Applications & Services*, 2008.

[80] Jan Nesvadba, P. Fonseca, A. Sinitsyn, F. de Lange, M. Thijssen, P. van Kaam, Hong Liu, R. van Leeuwen, J. Lukkien, A. Korostelev, Jan Ypma, B. Kroon, H. Celik, A. Hanjalic, U. Naci, J. Benois-Pineau, P. de With, and Jungong Han. Real-Time and Distributed AV Content Analysis System for

Consumer Electronics Networks. In *Proc. of International Conference on Multimedia and Expo*, pages 1549–1552. IEEE Computer Society, 2005.

[81] H. Neuroth, M. Kerzel, and W. Gentzsch, editors. *German Grid Initiative (D-Grid)*. Niedersächsische Staats- und Universitätsbibliothek, 2007. ISBN 3938616997.

[82] Henrik Frystyk Nielsen, Henry Sanders, Russell Butek, and Simon Nash. Direct Internet Message Encapsulation (DIME), 2002.

[83] S.D. Olabarriaga, P.T. De boer, Ketan Maheshwari, A. Belloum, J.G. Snel, A.J. Nederveen, and M. Bouwhuis. Virtual Lab for fMRI: Bridging the Usability Gap. In *Second IEEE International Conference on e-Science and Grid Computing (e-science 2006)*, 2006.

[84] Philippe Salembier. Overview of the MPEG-7 Standard and of Future Challenges for Visual Information Analysis. *EURASIP J. Appl. Signal Process.*, 2002(1):343–353, 2002.

[85] Paul Sandoz, Santiago Pericas-Geertsen, Kohuske Kawaguchi, Marc Hadley, and Eduardo Pelegri-Llopart. Fast Web Services, 2003. http://java.sun.com/developer/technicalArticles/WebServices/fastWS/.

[86] H. Schulzrinne, S. Casner, R. Frederick, and V. Jacobson. RTP: A Transport Protocol for Real-Time Applications, 2003. http://www.ietf.org/rfc/rfc3550.txt.

[87] Dominik Seiler, Steffen Heinzl, Ernst Juhnke, Ralph Ewerth, Manfred Grauer, and Bernd Freisleben. Efficient Data Transmission in Service Workflows for Distributed Video Content Analysis. In *Proceedings of the 6th International Conference on Advances in Mobile Computing & Multimedia*, pages 7–14. ACM Press and OCG Book Series, 2008.

[88] Balasubramanian Seshasayee, Karsten Schwan, and Patrick Widener. SOAP-binQ High-Performance SOAP with Continuous Quality Management. In *Proc. of the 24th Int'l. Conf. on Distributed Computing Systems*, pages 158–165, 2004.

[89] M. Smith, T. Friese, M. Engel, and B. Freisleben. Countering Security Threats in Service-Oriented On-Demand Grid Computing Using Sandboxing and Trusted Computing Techniques. *Journal of Parallel and Distributed Computing*, 66:1189–1204, 2006.

[90] Matthew Spencer, Renato Ferreira, Michael Beynon, Tahsin Kurc, Umit Catalyurek, Alan Sussman, and Joel Saltz. Executing Multiple Pipelined Data Analysis Operations in the Grid. In *Proceedings of the 2002*

ACM/IEEE conference on Supercomputing, pages 1–18, Los Alamitos, CA, USA, 2002. IEEE Computer Society Press.

[91] The Globus Alliance. GT Data Management: Reliable File Transfer (RFT), 2005. http://www.globus.org/toolkit/data/rft/.

[92] The GridSphere Project. GridSphere Portal Framework. http://www.gridsphere.org/.

[93] M. Tian, A. Gramm, H. Ritter, and J. Schiller. Efficient Selection and Monitoring of QoS-aware Web Services with the WS-QoS Framework. In *Proceedings of the IEEE/WIC/ACM International Conference on Web Intelligence (WI)*, pages 152–158, 2004.

[94] Vladimir Tosic, Abdelkarim Erradi, and Maheshwari Piyush. WS-Policy4MASC – A WS-Policy Extension Used in the MASC Middleware. In *Proc. of the IEEE International Conference on Services Computing (SCC)*, pages 458–465, 2007.

[95] Robert van Engelen, Gunjan Gupta, and Saurabh Pant. Developing Web Services for C and C++. *IEEE Internet Computing*, 7:53–61, 2003.

[96] Asir Vedamuthu, David Orchard, Frederick Hirsch, Maryann Hondo, Prasad Yendluri, Toufic Boubez, and Ümit Yalçinalp. Web Services Policy 1.5 – Framework. Technical report, W3C, 2007. http://www.w3.org/TR/2007/REC-ws-policy-20070904.

[97] Paul Viola and Michael J. Jones. Robust Real-Time Face Detection. *Int. J. Comput. Vision*, 57(2):137–154, 2004.

[98] Ying Ying, Yan Huang, and David W. Walker. A Performance Evaluation of Using SOAP with Attachments for e-Science. In *Proc. of the UK e-Science All Hands Meeting*, pages 796–803, 2005.

[99] Jin Yu, Boualem Benatallah, Fabio Casati, and Florian Daniel. Understanding Mashup Development. *IEEE Internet Computing*, 12(5):44–52, 2008.

[100] Hongwei Zeng and Huaikou Miao. Data Communication Model of Grid Workflow. In *ICEBE '06: Proceedings of the IEEE International Conference on e-Business Engineering*, pages 647–654, Washington, DC, USA, 2006. IEEE Computer Society.

Die VDM Verlagsservicegesellschaft sucht für wissenschaftliche Verlage abgeschlossene und herausragende

Dissertationen, Habilitationen, Diplomarbeiten, Master Theses, Magisterarbeiten usw.

für die kostenlose Publikation als Fachbuch.

Sie verfügen über eine Arbeit, die hohen inhaltlichen und formalen Ansprüchen genügt, und haben Interesse an einer honorarvergüteten Publikation?

Dann senden Sie bitte erste Informationen über sich und Ihre Arbeit per Email an *info@vdm-vsg.de*.

Sie erhalten kurzfristig unser Feedback!

VDM Verlagsservicegesellschaft mbH
Dudweiler Landstr. 99   Telefon +49 681 3720 174
D - 66123 Saarbrücken   Fax   +49 681 3720 1749
www.vdm-vsg.de

Die VDM Verlagsservicegesellschaft mbH vertritt

Printed by Books on Demand GmbH, Norderstedt / Germany